7/93

CONNIE CHUNG

Broadcast Journalist

Mary Malone

—**Contemporary Women Series**—

ENSLOW PUBLISHERS, INC.

Bloy St. and Ramsey Ave.   P.O. Box 38
Box 777   Aldershot
Hillside, N.J. 07205   Hants GU12 6BP
U.S.A.   U.K.

Library of Congress Cataloging-in-Publication Data

Malone, Mary.
  Connie Chung : broadcast journalist / Mary Malone.
    p. cm. — (Contemporary women series)
  Includes bibliographical references (p.) and index.
  ISBN 0-89490-332-2
  1. Chung, Connie. 2. Television journalists—United States—
Biography. 3. Television news anchors—United States—Biography.
4. Television broadcasting of news—United States. I. Title.
II. Series.
PN4874.C518M35 1992
070.4'092—dc20
[B]   91-25396
                                                          CIP

Printed in the United States of America

10 9 8 7 6 5 4 3 2 1

Illustration Credits:
Architect of the Capitol, Washington, D.C., p. 10; B'nai B'rith International, p. 71; College
of Journalism, University of Maryland at College Park, pp. 4, 16; Dwight D. Eisenhower
Library, p. 106; Gerald R. Ford Library, p. 61; Globe Photos, Inc., pp. 32, 90, 94; Jessica
Tandy and Hume Cronyn, photo by Roddy McDowell, p. 96; Jimmy Carter Library, p. 73;
Library of Congress, pp. 9, 42; Lyndon Baines Johnson Library, p. 108; Maryland Instruc-
tional Television, Producer of *Terra: Our World*, pp. 21, 67, 72; National Archives/Nixon
Project, pp. 44, 49; New York Public Library: United States History, Local History &
Genealogy Division-Astor, Lenox and Tilden Foundations, p. 80; Nielson Media Research,
p. 99; Norwich University, p. 55; Republican National Committee, p. 85; UPI/Bettmann
Newsphotos, pp. 38, 79, 104.

Cover Photo:
AP/Wide World Photos

921
CHUNG

Contents

Connie Chung

1

Saying Hello to Connie

"Tell Connie I said hello!"

That remark was often heard by the reporters of station KNXT in Los Angeles while Connie Chung was there. As the anchor of KNXT's local news, Connie became a familiar face on television. The people of the Los Angeles area liked her professional manner, her sincerity, and her warm smile. When she went out on stories herself, as she often did, she was greeted on all sides by a chorus of "Hi, Connie!" She became so popular in Los Angeles during the seven years she was there that her photograph, blown up, was used on KNXT's public advertisements.

Today, Connie's name and face are known nationwide. She is one of our foremost women broadcasters, but her fame did not come overnight. She paid her dues, as the saying goes, and now her name is like a signature to the shows she anchors, such as the recent *Saturday Night with Connie Chung,* and *Face to Face with Connie Chung.*

Connie had gone to California because it presented a challenge she could not resist. Anchoring not one but several local news programs for KNXT and at the same time raising their low ratings was her assignment. Such a task might have defeated another person, but Connie managed to do it.

It wasn't the first time in her career, nor the last, that Connie met and overcame obstacles. She was determined to succeed in the field she had chosen in college—television journalism. After graduation, a lucky break—the television industry's acceptance of affirmative action—got Connie a job as a rookie reporter with the CBS Washington, D.C., bureau. She was one of several minority persons hired at that time. Connie sometimes quipped about being selected through the government directive. She claimed she was a "double minority," Chinese and a woman, but it was her own drive and dedication to her work that carried her forward. As she advanced in her career, step by step, she never refused an assignment because it was too difficult or demanding.

During her Washington years, Connie was usually given the job of pinning down the hardest-to-get prominent political figures for interviews. After her California seasoning, Connie succeeded in winning a network news spot by accepting the grueling schedule of the earliest of morning shows, and as an established broadcaster she has continued with her dedication. Even when embarrassed by the failure of some of her specials, she does not give up. She is always ready to try something new.

Connie Chung's personal characteristics have been assets to her successful career. She is attractive and still appears youthful and vibrant after over twenty years in television. Slim and elegant, she is always dressed in good taste. Her sense of humor is well-known and livens up the interviews she gives as well as making her a popular guest on late-night shows. Many young people who are fans of David Letterman know Connie from her frequent appearances on his program.

Network news broadcasting and anchoring prime-time specials—that's Connie Chung's occupation, and she works hard at it. Many critics rate her on a par with Barbara Walters. Connie's success is an example of the fulfillment of the American dream. Besides being a star in her own right, she has been called the best-known Chinese-American of her generation.

2

China to America

In 1944, the Chung family of Shanghai, China, prepared to leave for the United States. China had been under attack by Japan for several years, long before the United States entered World War II after the bombing of Pearl Harbor. The United States then became an ally of China and provided that besieged country with military aid and supplies. America's help, however, was given to the Nationalist party, headed by General Chiang Kai-shek, not to the Communists, led by Mao Tse-tung. Civil war between the factions would grow even more bitter after World War II ended. Eventually, the Communists won the support of the majority of the people, and Mao would establish the People's Republic of China.

In the early 1940s, however, living conditions in China were appalling, especially in the crowded cities like Shanghai. There were acute shortages of food, which would lead to famine in a few years; the factories and warehouses, along with most other buildings, had been destroyed; the hospitals lacked medicines and doctors. Malnutrition and disease were widespread. Children were particularly susceptible. Five of William and Margaret Chung's children died in infancy. Four daughters were left, and their parents were determined to save them.

Because Mr. Chung belonged to the Nationalist party, which the United States supported, he had connections in Washington, D.C. The Chung daughters would have a better life in the United States, he was sure. Women in China were not yet considered equal to men. Not until the People's Republic was established in 1949 would Chinese women be accorded a higher status—encouraged to prepare for professional careers and do whatever men could do. Before that time, however, marriage was considered the only acceptable course for girls, and marriages were arranged by parents. William Chung and his future wife had never seen each other until the day of their wedding. The marriage was a happy one, though, and their children—all girls—were cherished.

A view of Shanghai, China, where the Chung family lived before coming to America.

The Chungs' dangerous escape from war-torn Shanghai was accomplished successfully. They were taken aboard a ship leaving the port of Shanghai for America and arrived safely in Washington where William Chung obtained a position in the Chinese diplomatic service. Later, he joined the Washington, D.C., branch of the United Nations. The family was able to settle in one of the pleasant suburbs of the nation's capital. There, on August 20, 1946, another child was born to the Chungs—a daughter, the last of their ten children and the first born in America. It was she who was destined to bring honor to the Chung family name.

The new daughter's name was decided by the Chungs' four older daughters. After their father called them from the hospital

Washington, D.C., seat of the United States government, became the Chungs' new home.

announcing the birth of the baby, the girls got out one of their favorite movie magazines as a source for names. No more American method of naming children could they have chosen. "Okay," said the oldest girl, who was fifteen, "the first page we turn to is going to be her." The first picture of a movie actress they saw in *Photoplay* magazine was one of Constance Moore. "Oh, was I lucky," Connie Chung says now. "It could have been a real disaster."

Ironically, Connie is more famous than the movie actress for whom she was named; she herself became a brighter star than any other in the old movie magazines her sisters treasured.

Although she was named by her sisters and is known to millions as simply Connie Chung, Connie has another name also. In *Who's Who in America,* she has listed herself as Constance Yu-Hwa Chung, as if to emphasize her Chinese birthright. Connie's Chinese name, given to her by her parents, can be translated as "Precious Ivory" Chung.

As a young child, Connie, the baby of the family, was bossed by her older sisters. They were a talkative, opinionated group who outvoted Connie on most issues. There are certain disadvantages in being the youngest in a large family as such children know. Besides feeling somewhat intimidated by her older sisters, Connie also had to put up with their teasing. They called her "hwa-chow," a Chinese term for foreigner. In her early years, Connie was bothered by that. She said she felt inferior because she was the only one of her family not born in China. Of course, she spoke Chinese, the language spoken at home by all the Chungs. But Connie wanted very much to be one of the group, she said, able to share common memories of their Chinese homeland. She loved to hear the stories the older Chungs told about China. Her sisters' teasing, although good-natured, sometimes made Connie felt like an outsider.

However, most of Connie's memories of childhood and adolescence are happy ones. "We were a big, wonderful family," she says. There were parties and picnics with friends from the Chinese diplomatic circles William Chung was associated with as well as neighbors in the prosperous suburb of Washington.

By 1949 the Chungs realized they would never return to Shanghai. It was clear that Mao Tse-tung's Communist party was in control of China. As followers of Chiang Kai-shek, the family's lives would be endangered by returning. The Chungs instead became United States citizens and loyal Americans.

Of all her sisters, Connie was closest to the next youngest one, Maimie. It was Maimie who, having sided with her older sisters about giving Connie an American name, then tried to help her little sister become Americanized. She told her as much as she could about the public school all the Chung girls attended. But Connie was shy and, compared to her young classmates, very quiet. One of her teachers in elementary school wrote on her report card, "Speaks too softly." Reading that, Connie was devastated and ran home crying. Her mother comforted her by reminding her that with four older sisters, it was natural for Connie to speak softly. The older girls were always talking—and not very softly. As the youngest and the baby, Connie was used to being out-talked by her sisters and often couldn't get a word in even if she wanted to. She was almost forced to be quiet and meek, she recalled.

Connie had been especially upset by her teacher's remark because it was always her way, even as a young child, to try to be perfect. She called herself "a regular goody-two-shoes." If speaking up and speaking out was what her teacher thought desirable, Connie would try to improve.

But she found it hard to adapt while she was in elementary school. The children acted so differently from what was considered a well-behaved Chinese youngster. These American children were noisy, even boisterous at times. Often Connie felt so overwhelmed by their high spirits that she would go off by herself, pick up a book, and pretend to study—not that she needed to study. School work was never a problem for her. Even if she had not wanted to excel,

12

.

maybe preferring to be one of the "regular kids," Connie knew her parents expected her to do well. The Chinese tradition of high regard for education was upheld in the Chung family. Both parents believed that a good education was the surest way to success in America. Like so many other Chinese people, the Chungs encouraged their children to study hard and to prepare themselves for college. Advanced degrees were not impossible. In fact, they would help young people obtain first-class positions and be free from the discrimination that ignorance and lack of education might encourage.

Quiet and meek though she might have been, Connie already showed early signs of what she would like to do later. Television was a great educator—for better or worse—for her as it is for almost all young people. What seemed to impress Connie most was the way the news commentators and reporters interviewed people. Her mother recalls that when Connie was only four, she started to use the metal tube from a vacuum cleaner as a make-believe microphone to "interview" friends.

The traditionally strict Chinese work ethic prevailed in the Chung household as well as the respect for education. All of the sisters helped with the housework, even Connie, who was not very good at it and not at all domestic. She never learned to cook as her sisters did. Once, when she was a television personality, Connie says she decided to prepare a dinner in honor of her mother's birthday. The stew she cooked for twelve hours turned out to be a disaster. Her mother was sympathetic, though. "Never mind, dear," she commented, "You were meant to do the news."

However, Connie did learn to sew very well, probably because of her interest in clothes. She loved to dress up and loved shopping for new outfits. For years, even when she was in college, she made all of her own clothes. As a television star, she won recognition for her good taste in dressing, her beautifully tailored suits, her striking accessories. Conservative but elegant has been her style.

Connie, as a young girl, did not feel that she was at all attractive. She was tiny and "skinny," as she said, and from the side, "I looked like a small letter L with long feet when I wore flats." She did not develop physically as soon as the other girls in her public school class. That changed, of course, by the time she reached high school, and she decided she was not going to be the quiet, meek little girl her sisters knew. She became active in student government and took part in her high school plays and shows. She was in a school with a great many gifted and talented students, many of them the children of Washington VIPs. Goldie Hawn, the future actress, and Carl Bernstein, who would become a famous reporter, were classmates of Connie Chung.

It was when Connie was in high school that her sister Maimie decided to teach the younger girl how to apply eye makeup. If there was one thing that drew attention to the two of them as Chinese, it was their eyes. Those round Chinese eyes, Connie has said, looked "right off the boat." Maimie was willing to teach Connie how to use eyeliner, eyebrow pencil, and eyeshadow. The parents allowed the girls to experiment, understanding their desire to look more American. Connie was an apt pupil in learning to apply the makeup and, after seeing the difference it made, never omitted it in any public appearance.

Even in high school, Connie was interested in the workings of the government. The students were raised on the *Washington Post* newspaper, Connie remembers, and kept abreast of what was happening on Capitol Hill. "You can't grow up in Washington, D.C., and not be extremely aware of what's going on," she told an interviewer in later years. "It's part of local news in addition to being network news. You can't grow up like I did without developing an interest for how this country works." Being close to the seat of government, the students often saw Washington bigwigs on the local news, even on the streets. Visits to Capitol Hill and meeting

Congressmen became part of the high school's civics and history courses.

A great many of Connie's high school friends continued their education at the nearby College Park campus of the University of Maryland. That's where she enrolled, also, and entered in September 1965. She decided on biology as her major.

In college, Connie came far out of her meek shell and was so popular that she was elected freshman queen. By this time, she was very attractive, although she never claimed more than being, as she said, "decent-looking." Her small, five-foot three-inch figure, elevated always by spike heels, was trim and graceful. Connie had lustrous black hair and a smooth complexion; her dark eyes, of course, were highlighted by the eye makeup that she jokingly claimed transformed her from a "refugee/boat person into someone who was finally presentable."

Between her junior and senior years in college, Connie obtained a job as a summer intern in the office of New York Congressman Seymour Halpern. He had been a newspaperman, and he encouraged Connie to try her hand at writing speeches and press releases. She discovered that she enjoyed that type of work. "That's when I got bitten by the bug," she says. "It was a lot of fun writing and watching the reporters doing their thing . . . it was the first time I sort of watched politics at work."

When she returned to the university for her senior year, she switched her major to journalism. "I couldn't see spending my life in a laboratory," she said—certainly not after the excitement of watching politics at work and seeing the television reporters' participation in that hectic lifestyle. "Dissecting frogs lost its appeal," she said.

Connie did so well in her journalism courses that she was awarded a certificate of recognition for outstanding scholarship. She regretted having to concentrate on the journalism courses and not having time for the academic subjects she felt could have given her background knowledge for her news reports. However, she was always an avid reader and never had trouble learning what she had to know before discussing any subject on television.

While a senior in college, Connie thought she would try to get a head start on a future position in television reporting—her objective after she graduated. She decided she wanted a career in broadcast journalism because she believed television was growing and newspapers waning. Connie described her job search: "I went around to all the stations in Washington and asked for any available

As a journalism senior in college, Connie received a certificate of recognition for outstanding scholarship.

job." At one of the stations where she applied, WTTG, a Metrome-dia television station in Washington, she was told there was no opening available. But shortly afterward, the news director called Connie at home and said, "After you left I told the rest of the staff you were looking for a job but we had no openings, and they offered to take up a collection if I hired you."

She started at WTTG as a part-time copygirl for two nights a week. Her job was something like all-around odd-jobs girl. Connie was willing to take on any task in order to be near the media. "She desperately wanted a job in broadcasting," the news director said. Stamina and determination—those two qualities displayed early—would characterize Connie Chung's successful career.

Connie worked at WTTG on a part-time basis until she graduated from college in 1969. She was ready then, as she imagined, for the big time.

3

Television "Brat"

With her part-time job at WTTG, Connie Chung already had one foot in the door of television reporting. However, that was only the beginning. Connie's objective was to become a full-fledged reporter, not to stay as a copygirl for very long. After her graduation from college, she made the rounds of the television stations in Washington that were affiliated with the big national systems. She was turned down by all of them. At CBS, William Small, the director of the news department, told her to "come back in ten years."

After Connie graduated, she was offered full-time work at WTTG with just a slight change in title. She would be "copy clerk" instead of copygirl. Connie disliked anything considered "typically female," so that was an improvement, and because she couldn't obtain anything better, she accepted WTTG's offer. It wasn't very long before a further small step upward became possible. A newsroom secretary's position opened up, and Connie was asked if she wanted that job. She decided that although a secretary was a "female" type of position, it would put her closer to the news. She consented to take it, and she acted as secretary while still doing everything possible to get into reporting of the news. In a small local station like WTTG, there was a good deal of overlapping of job duties.

"I did a lot of research and stuff like that," Connie said. "And I'd always volunteer. Send me, you know, send me . . . When they did, once in a while, I'd take notes and I'd come back with all the information and write it for the anchorman. Or else I would try to send myself out on stories. I'd call in and I'd set something up where I knew they didn't have anybody. I just kept trying to get myself out there and reporting."

"She worked on us constantly," said Stan Berk, the director of news at WTTG. She was, according to him, "always imploring 'Please let me write.' Slowly, we began to let her go out on interviews. Then she learned to splice tapes. Finally, we made her a full-fledged reporter." That happened just as soon as there was an opening for a writer-reporter. Connie had, of course, been waiting eagerly for it.

The news director behaved cautiously, however. Connie was told they would "try her out." Her youth and her family background, which she herself described as a "sheltered Chinese home," made it seem likely to the men in the business that she would not be able to withstand the rugged, almost cutthroat competition that characterized television reporting. Running after newsmakers, struggling to get up front with a microphone through a crowd of rival reporters, and participating in the shouted exchanges with the celebrity of the moment were all part of the reporters' daily work. They accepted it, however, as Connie knew and as she would herself.

Besides her trial status, there was another string attached to Connie's promotion. She would still have to do the secretarial work because a replacement had not been found. But she rebelled. "No, no, no," she said "I don't want to do that anymore. I want to be a writer."

In her own rapid, headlong style, Connie related how she found her own replacement. "I went across the street to this bank, and there was this really cute black teller who used to cash my checks, and I said, 'Toni, can you type?' And she said, 'Yeah.' And I said, 'You want to be a big star at that TV station across the street?' She said, 'Sure.' She got the job, and so did I."

The young lady who took Connie's job became a television producer with WTTG some time later.

Yet, even with her promotion to writer, Connie still didn't get enough air time to satisfy her. Because she was the youngest and the most recent recruit in the reporters' corps, she was often passed over when it came to getting credit. Even when she had written the material on a story she went after, someone else might read it on the air.

This went on for a while until Connie decided to do something about it. With a year and a half now of television experience, she went around again to the other stations. Finally, she "finagled" (one of her favorite words) an offer from the ABC affiliate station in Washington for an on-the-air reporting job. Then she returned to her WTTG bosses and told them of ABC's offer. What she hoped would happen did. She recalls that they said, "No, don't leave. We'll put you on the air."

Connie says frankly, "I coerced them." But she did go on the air after that and appeared often on the ten o'clock news. She enjoyed her new job. Only 24 years old, she met, as she says, all the network people, especially the executives, and they got to know her and watched her work. She became known as a reporter who didn't "let go," as Richard Salant, the president of CBS, described her tenacity in interviewing people.

As an on-the-air reporter, Connie covered all kinds of stories. Antiwar demonstrations were common in Washington at that time because of the feeling against the war in Vietnam, and Connie covered them as well as crime, disasters, and whatever Congressional investigations were going on. She did not always enjoy the grimmer aspects of some of her stories, but as she said, she'd "plow through and get there anyway." No longer did the television executives fear that Connie Chung couldn't hack it with her competitors.

Although she appeared tiny beside the mostly male crowd of reporters on any big story, Connie did not allow herself to be brushed aside. She learned quite soon that even though she didn't like it, she had to push and shove her way to the front. Wherever the story or the celebrity was, Connie did her best to get close. "She was small and pretty but she could elbow with the best of them," *Newsweek* magazine reported.

Connie's "old-fashioned" Chinese relatives, she said, did not always approve of the "callous" behavior she had to adopt in order to get some of her stories. It was un-Chinese, they told her. But

Connie Chung as a young television reporter.

Connie maintained that she was different at home. Being aggressive was not her nature, it was just a necessary quality for a reporter to have. She could joke about it, too. "Give me a tear-gas, rock-throwing riot any time," she said.

Connie left WTTG not long after she became a full-fledged reporter. She was "on a roll," as her fellow worker at the station, Maury Povich, would say. Connie secretly admired young Mr. Povich. He was so sure of himself, so handsome (he looked like the movie actor George Segal, she thought). Maury was an experienced reporter, a real "star." He was the host, then, of WTTG's midday talk show *Panorama*. "I used to sit there and watch in awe as he was just ripping copy out of the typewriter," Connie remembers. She said to him once. "Oh, Mr. Povich, how do you write so well and so fast?"

Maury didn't pay much attention to Connie. He was married, successful, busy. Like Connie, he too was a "D.C. brat," born in Washington and brought up in a "news-saturated" community dependent on government activities and Congressional events. His father was a long-time sports writer for the *Washington Post*. Maury had gone away for his college training and graduated in 1962 from the University of Pennsylvania. Six years older than Connie, he was far above her in status and importance in the television station. Their relationship at WTTG, never more than that of casual acquaintances, ended when their paths separated a few years later and they lost touch with each other. Each of them went on to bigger television systems, Maury to the NBC affiliate in Chicago, Connie to CBS in Washington.

Connie Chung was nearly 25 when she left WTTG in 1971. Being hired by CBS television's Washington bureau was a really big break. She had applied there again for the job of reporter at exactly the right time. Greater opportunity in television was opening for women and minorities due to the pressure being exerted by the Federal Communications Commission, which oversees the television industry. The networks were advised to take affirmative action seriously and begin employing more women—men already dominated the field—and more ethnic minorities.

Connie has related many times, with humor as well as frankness, what happened when she applied the second time at CBS. "They had only one woman at CBS News at the time and they wanted to hire more. So they hired me, they hired Lesley Stahl, they hired Michele Clark, and they hired Sylvia Chase . . . In other words, a Chinese woman, a black woman, a nice Jewish girl, and a blond shiksa [the Jewish term for Gentile]. Perfect. And so they took care of years of discrimination."

With Connie's drive and ability, it is not likely that her rise in television was due to preferential treatment because she was a double minority—Chinese and a woman. However, affirmative action helped her at the time she was trying to establish a base in a field that had previously been very difficult for the minority groups to enter. Afterward, when she was well known in television, she was often asked how it was possible that such a young Chinese female could have risen so far. Even one of the executives at CBS posed such a question. Connie took it lightly and told him it was because Bill Small (the news director, her immediate boss) liked the way she did his shirts. She explained her sometimes flippant answers by remarking that "Americans always think Chinese people own restaurants and laundries, you know, which I've had to live with all my life. I usually don't get perturbed." Her robust sense of humor helped her remain unfazed by the attention caused by her Chinese appearance. She made fun of it and herself. After she was successfully established in the media, she referred to herself as television's best known "yellow journalist."

Nevertheless, Connie sometimes worried that her appearance did distract her television audiences. They would see her come on the screen, and they might remark, "Look, she's Chinese." At the network, where she said she really had to push herself to be aggressive, some people called her the "Dragon Lady." She was philosophical about it all, however, explaining that news "has to make you hard." It is certainly true that covering shoot-outs for the local news quite understandably gives reporters a real taste of the underside of life.

Because she had done local news for WTTG, Connie was pretty well-known in Washington when she started at CBS. The *Washington Post* wrote that CBS "pulled a real coup" in hiring her. Although all of the networks were "scrambling for their token Chinese," the article continued, "Connie Chungs are not to be found under every tree."

William Small, the CBS executive who had hired several women newscasters at the same time as Connie Chung, denied hiring anybody for any reason except competence and ability to produce the best newscasts. In the case of women being hired, he said "CBS does not employ pretty faces."

As it turned out, many of the women and minorities hired by CBS in the early 1970s established themselves as excellent broadcasters. Lesley Stahl became a White House correspondent and well known through her nightly reports on the CBS Evening News. Michele Clark, black, and thus a double minority like Connie Chung, was assigned to the CBS Morning News in the network's affiliate station in Chicago. Two black men hired by CBS around the same time as Connie became very successful broadcasters: Ed Bradley on *60 Minutes* and Bernard Shaw, now an anchorman on the CNN network news.

In the big league of television broadcasting, CBS was at that time considered the foremost news-gathering network in the country. Connie was determined to make good in what she called her "dream job." She was ready to accept any assignment given her. Dan Rather was a reporter covering the White House then, and he was impressed by Connie's attitude. "You couldn't be around her for five seconds and not know that she was willing to do anything," he said. "No assignment was too gritty or grimy, no weather was too inclement to send her out." William Small, who had once told Connie to come back in ten years, felt the same way about Connie's driving work ethic, which she herself playfully attributed to her Chinese ancestry.

CBS had some big names, known nationally, in its news department. Connie looked, listened, and learned from them. Besides Dan Rather, there was Roger Mudd, who reported from Capitol Hill, Marvin Kalb in the State Department, Bob Shiefer at the Pentagon, and Daniel Schorr, who covered the other federal agencies. All of them, however, reported to Walter Cronkite, the top newsman of CBS, the final authority. For many of his audience he was "the most trusted man in America." From his headquarters in New York City, Cronkite shaped the CBS news department. He always thoroughly checked all the reports coming in to him and decided which of them were worthy of attention. Occasionally, a junior reporter like Connie would contribute a story that rated a "spot" of thirty seconds on the evening news.

However, Connie, along with her contemporaries Lesley Stahl and Ed Bradley, absorbed valuable lessons from the "big guys." The "youngsters" sat at their desks in the hallway at the CBS studio and watched and listened when they were not hard at work writing assigned stories. "There were firm rules on how to build a news story," Connie recalls, "and I learned how to do things right. Those formative years as a reporter, under the traditional, credible CBS approach to getting enough sources to do a story, were critical to my development."

In the beginning at CBS, while she was still a rookie, Connie might be the second reporter on a news story. "One of the heavy hitters like Dan Rather would do the evening news piece," said Ed Fouhy, the Washington bureau chief. Connie would do the radio and morning news stories. She was soon recognized at CBS as a real asset to the news department—"motivated, determined, a very hard-working young lady."

Along with the basics of writing news stories, there were other lessons Connie learned in her "dream job." For instance, she said, "like what to do with your hair and where to go for makeup advice." The eye makeup was still essential to her appearance, she believed. "I look very different without my eyes," she said jokingly.

Connie has agreed with some of the women broadcasters' complaints about the attention paid to their appearance. The public is more severe in judging the women's looks than they are with men. Makeup and hairdos are closely watched. It seems that people—and the television executives—are willing to accept ordinary-looking men but want more glamour in the women broadcasters, and maybe consider looks more important than the women's reporting skills. Also, the women on television claim they are required to look youthful and are demoted after their years of youth and good looks are over, while the men can go on for years longer, as Walter Cronkite did.

About the question of women and youth on television, Connie has as usual treated it lightly. In her own case, she said, "Chinese people don't age very fast. Chinese women hold their age well." When asked why, Connie replied with a smile, "We Chinese are inscrutable," and referring to another widely held belief about Orientals, she said, "We all look alike, you know."

Few women, however, have stayed in television news broadcasting for the length of time that men have. Pauline Frederick is possibly the best example of a long-lasting female reporter. She was on network news for 12 years, reporting regularly from the United Nations. She had been told at one time that a woman's voice lacked authority. As late as 1972, NBC executive Reuven Frank told a reporter, "I have the strong feeling that audiences are less prepared to accept news from a woman's voice than a man's." However,

Pauline Frederick's popularity and her high standing in audience acceptance seemed to contradict Frank's theory.

But such feelings die hard. At the CBS Washington bureau, three of the young women appointed in 1971—Connie Chung, Lesley Stahl, and Marya McLaughlin—did not appear often on *CBS Evening News* in their first years but could be said to be serving their apprenticeship under the more experienced newsmen. The star reporters were still the men who formed Walter Cronkite's "supporting cast."

At CBS, Connie learned something that many news commentators had denied in the early days of news broadcasting. By this time, after Barbara Walters' breakthrough, it was recognized that television news really is show business and that newscasters are performers, not merely readers of material. Connie Chung has never denied for an instant that television news is show business. "Anybody who's in television is on an ego trip," she said early in her career when interviewed by a *Washington Post* reporter. "I think you would find that people who thought of being in the theatre or politics many times end up in television. There has to be showmanship."

A distinguished journalist, Frank Mankiewicz, who was political director of Senator McGovern's 1972 presidential campaign, explained what made television news "show business." He said that a newspaper's main job is to provide news; "television's main job is to entertain." He continued: "Newspapers usually try to give as much news as possible, while television stations generally offer as little news as possible."

Ben Bradlee, editor of the *Washington Post,* when asked why people trust television news more than newspapers, said it was because television comes "coated, and in very small doses, and it disappears." Admitting the power and the immediacy of television news, he claimed that it is over once it disappears, but with a

27

newspaper, one can go back, reread, and maybe see an explanatory map that is right there with the article.

Since Mankiewicz and Bradlee commented on television news, several cable networks devoted to news only have sprung up. But to many watchers of the evening news, it still appears that a whole newspaper's amount of news may be condensed into a half-hour time slot on television.

Connie learned that the image, not just the appearance alone, that a news broadcaster projected was important. Audiences were very much aware of it and proved that by phone calls to the station if they had criticisms of any performer, newscasters as well as entertainment figures. Connie commented that it all came together on the show—the voice, the look, the delivery as well as the style of writing. As a writer, Connie was very much concerned about adapting her writing skills to the television screen. "It takes a long time to develop good style, and television writing is a little different," she said. "It has to be less convoluted or no one will understand it. I write my sentences too long sometimes, and then I run out of breath."

Running out of breath can be a disaster, as Connie learned once during an assignment. She had overslept one morning and had to rush to the building where the Senate judiciary hearings connected with the Watergate case were being held. When she got there, she found the elevator out of order and had to run up several flights of stairs. As soon as she arrived in the committee room, she said, "They put the mike on me, and all I could do was pant."

In order to get stories, a television reporter has to learn how to approach people. Connie has admitted that even with her valuable training at CBS in Washington, it was quite a while before she mastered that difficult technique. "It's really hard to finagle stories out of people," she has said, "It's important how you phrase your questions . . . Even when an approach is successful, it doesn't always come across." With a restricted time limit, she continued,

"You can't get into the mood and character in depth . . . How can you possibly get a mood out of forty-five seconds?"

Connie Chung has been characterized in many articles as having broken into television broadcasting without any journalistic experience. That, however, is a criticism that is unfounded because, as she herself said, the best way to learn journalism is "on the job," and that is how she learned at CBS—the graduate school of broadcast journalism. After her first years at CBS, Connie knew how to get a story, how to put it together, and how to present it effectively on the air.

4

An American Journey

Connie's first really big assignment as a CBS network correspondent was to cover the campaign of one of the 1972 Democratic presidential hopefuls. George McGovern, a senator from South Dakota, was preparing to challenge several others in the primary elections that would take place in the winter and spring of 1972. McGovern was an avowed liberal, an opponent of the Vietnam War, and a critic of the corruption in government.

Presidential candidates start hitting the campaign trail at least a year before election time. In 1972, the Republican party's 1968 winner, Richard Nixon, was in the White House and as was customary for presidents, he would be his party's candidate for reelection. He was so well known already, after 25 years in public office, that he felt he did not have to campaign. Most of the action, the newspapers agreed, would be on the Democratic side.

From the beginning, Senator McGovern's campaign was considered hopeless by practically all of the political experts. Nevertheless, CBS decided that it would prove an ideal training ground for their promising young reporters who needed seasoning. Connie Chung, and Michele Clark, who had been hired at the same time as

Connie, were both assigned to cover Senator McGovern. Michele's home base was the Chicago bureau of CBS. She was described by Timothy Crouse in his book *The Boys on the Bus* as "a young, extremely beautiful black reporter." He added that she was proving to be an excellent correspondent, even though she herself said, "I think they're just letting me get my feet wet."

Michele and Connie worked together covering Senator McGovern's campaign until after the second primary. In Wisconsin, Michele was assigned to Hubert Humphrey, the former vice president under President Lyndon Johnson, now hopeful of winning his party's presidential nomination. But after the Wisconsin primary, Humphrey began losing to McGovern, and soon he withdrew from the race. Michele returned to the CBS "Morning News" television program in Chicago, but her promising career tragically ended when she died in a plane crash at Chicago's Midway Airport in November 1972.

Connie was a rookie when she started on the campaign trek with the McGovern organization. She was the "number-three person" CBS had assigned to the campaign, the "low man on the totem pole," she said. She would be expected to file reports that might end up on CBS radio, or more luckily, on the early morning show. A senior correspondent would file for Walter Cronkite's prime-time evening news broadcast.

Whatever the television reporters transmitted to their networks, it could be condensed by one of the "big guys"—Walter Cronkite or Roger Mudd—into a twenty-second spot on the *CBS Evening News*. That was one of the realities of long-distance reporting. There was also the necessity of locating good visuals, pictures that went with a story. People who were willing to talk on camera were a plus, too. Without the visuals and the voices, even the best-written piece would most likely be "killed."

Roger Mudd had been through the system. Although now one of the CBS star correspondents assigned to Capitol Hill, he under-

Connie Chung was assigned by CBS to cover the McGovern campaign.

stood the drawbacks of campaign reporting. "You've got all that claptrap equipment," he said. He likened it—the camera and its crew—to a ball and chain, which was bound to hamper the television reporter from getting to a story fast.

In the beginning of her career as a television reporter, Connie Chung was unaware of how experienced reporters often got their information. After missing some stories, she learned that the men reporters had a network of sources that led them to breaking news events. Ruefully, Connie realized that she was not "plugged in to everything." Using sources might be a casual thing, but it produced results. Roger Mudd could have lunch with McGovern's speech writer; Bruce Morton, another experienced correspondent, might know the Senator's political director; Mike Wallace had many contacts with newspapermen. The big names in the media as well as the press could always seem to get closer to the candidate himself.

Of course, with her characteristic will to succeed, Connie decided to cultivate her own sources. To further that aim, she started to take in the parties and the after-hours and behind-the-scenes social affairs where connections to the network were often formed. Once the other reporters got to know Connie, they accepted her and before long, respected her for her dedication to her job.

After Connie realized how essential connections were, she made it a rule to cultivate important people who could help her to advance her career. Sometimes, however, she was overeager to claim "friendship" with certain persons. An unfortunate experience in later years with New York City's then mayor, Edward Koch, is such an example. While with NBC, Connie pressed for an interview with Mayor Koch on the subject of dumping sludge in the ocean. He would be pitted against an expert who was expected to be critical of the city's dumping policy. The mayor at first refused to give the interview unless his own expert, the city's environmental protection director, Harvey Schultz, could be interviewed with him. Connie agreed, but when the program was aired, the director's part had been cut out. Koch was furious and called it "a breach of journalistic ethics."

But at the age of 26 on McGovern's campaign, Connie was still new, still a rookie, and going on such a political trip was an exciting experience. She declared it was the best breaking-in a raw reporter could have. Besides, she got to know the United States as only a campaigner could. Even to Senator McGovern, that 1972 political journey was "a great opportunity to know this country as you can know it in no other way." He led what was probably the most grueling campaign in American history.

The modern primary elections have supplanted the old raucous convention balloting in the stifling convention halls of pre-airconditioned times. The party leaders or bosses sometimes would make deals in their smoke-filled rooms and next day would present their candidate to the convention delegates. Through the bosses' influence, the delegates usually were forced to accept someone perhaps unknown to them, a dark horse, or an unpopular figure. Now, through the primary elections, voters in each party in each state have the say about what candidates they prefer. Television can be said to favor the present method by staging media events at some state primaries, and by a coverage of candidates that goes on for months. The entrants in a primary are constantly subjected to the scrutiny of the cameras and the questions of reporters. The method may be tough for the candidates, but it does succeed in making them well known to the public.

Starting in February in snowy New Hampshire, the presidential hopefuls appear in person and on the ballots. They solicit votes on street corners, outside factories, on courthouse steps. The final winner is the one who stays the course in all of the primary elections, coming out on top in the crucial ones. Losers drop out along the way. The winner is practically assured of nomination at the party convention in the summer.

Campaign reporters were assigned by CBS and the other television networks to cover a single candidate for as long as he was in the race. They soon got to know the candidate so well they often identified with him and were disappointed at his setbacks. When a candidate did poorly in a few primaries and dropped out, the reporter who had covered him would most likely be assigned to another hopeful still in the contest. Connie stayed with front-runner Senator McGovern all the way. She would continue to cover him as the presidential candidate after he won in the primary elections.

Now as the presidential election drew near, the campaign would really heat up. This was the big time—the contest between the two parties and their nominees—not an elimination trial within a party. Senator McGovern, before he was finished, would travel over 50,000 miles criss-crossing the country, making repeated visits in critical areas. Accompanied by his staff and the media, he made stops in more than 200 cities in forty states. After he won the primaries, two United Airlines planes were charted by McGovern's staff to carry all the personnel involved. Before, they had traveled mostly by bus.

When they rode on the bus, the wire service reporters from the Associated Press (AP) and the United Press International (UPI) and the television cameramen sat up front so they could get out fast. The wire service reporters especially had hard schedules to meet. They dashed for the telephones at every stop in order to call in their bulletins. Anything and everything that happened on the campaign trail would be transmitted by the wire services. They in turn supplied the countless newspapers across the nation that depended on the services for political news. The big daily papers, like *The New York Times* and the *Washington Post,* had their own political reporters. These and all other reporters—from news magazines as well as the media networks—sat in the mid-section of the bus. McGovern staff members sat in the rear, usually busy with plans for the next stop.

Of the two airplanes chartered by McGovern's staff, the first was named *Dakota Queen II* after the B24 bomber McGovern had piloted in World War II. This plane carried the Senator and his chief aides. Only 34 seats were reserved for the media, and those were occupied by the biggest names from all of the news-gathering agencies. Those who didn't rate the *Dakota Queen II* rode on the second plane, called the *Zoo* because it was so crowded.

Connie traveled along with the other reporters, either on the bus or on the *Zoo* plane. *The Boys on the Bus* by Timothy Crouse, one of several books that came out of the 1972 campaign, referred to Connie Chung as "the pretty Chinese CBS correspondent." Crouse indicated that Connie was very much on the ball. He noticed her especially because she had the room next to his at the hotel in Los Angeles where they were lodged. He was impressed because Connie got up early, "bright and alert" in order to get a statement of some kind from Senator McGovern before the other reporters. Connie was used to getting up early. She often arrived at McGovern's house in Washington—when he was there—at 5:00 A.M. so as not to miss him. Dan Rather noticed when he was with the McGovern campaign that Connie was "right at McGovern's elbow every possible second." If the Senator gave a breakfast speech somewhere, Connie would dictate short sections of it into her Sony before it was time to run for the bus.

Other reporters on the campaign also observed Connie's tenacity. CBS correspondent Bob Schieffer remembered that "George McGovern used to say there wasn't a morning he didn't wake up to find Connie Chung waiting around the corner with a microphone. She was driven, always doing an extra spot late at night, never afraid to ask a tough question."

Some people might consider such a life as the campaign reporters lived while on assignment as too uncomfortable, too removed from reality. Arriving at hotels in strange cities late at night, hurried meals, never getting enough sleep before it was time to start out again—that was the life of "the boys on the bus." When they were "the boys on the plane," it wasn't much better being crowded into the *Zoo,* where everyone ate, worked, and napped. And of course, they all had to find time to write, record, and file their reports for the next day's news stories. Naturally they grumbled, but if they were like Connie, they considered themselves lucky to have such exciting jobs.

Even listening to and reporting on McGovern's speeches did not dull Connie's enthusiasm for her participation with the press contingent. Boredom was not allowed to show, even after listening to the same speeches given over and over at airports, city intersections, hotel ballrooms to labor unions, veterans' groups, senior citizens, local politicians, whatever.

Although Senator McGovern was considered by many of his followers to be a superb campaigner in the "people-to-people" manner, he was not especially effective on television. In 1972, the old-style campaigning that worked for Harry Truman in 1948 was outmoded. Media coverage had come to be far more important in political campaigns than the earlier method of touring the country by rail and addressing audiences from the back of the train.

Senator McGovern was described in a very uncomplimentary way in *Newsweek* magazine. "His eyes go flat and lifeless on television. His voice struggles for passion . . . he looks less the politician than the schoolmaster." Although the senator had put together a strong campaign organization, it was acknowledged even by his own people that the media is far more important than organization in a presidential campaign. And although he did receive a great deal of media coverage, mainly because President Nixon did not campaign, McGovern failed to come across as "presidential." He seemed to many people to be incompetent, indecisive. This seemed particularly so when he first supported Senator Thomas Eagleton, his running mate who had been treated for emotional problems, then wavered and dropped him off the ticket. McGovern's moral outrage over the Vietnam War and our military involvement in Indochina was not then shared by most of the people. Later, both that prolonged, unpopular war and the Watergate scandal that toppled President Nixon would make many of Senator McGovern's issues seem justifiable.

But in 1972, in spite of his "nice guy" reputation, McGovern was not completely trusted by the majority of voters. He wanted to enlist under his banner several groups that had been left out of the political mainstream. Young people, women, blacks, and other minorities were appealed to and were promised greater participation in government if he was elected. For that and for some of his other proposals, McGovern was considered a radical—too far left for most Americans. His plan to give amnesty to draft dodgers and his income redistribution idea to benefit the poor aroused much

Presidential candidate George McGovern on a campaign stop.

opposition. Also, his attempt to build an image as someone with a higher code of conduct than most politicians did not appeal to many voters. The *Washington Post* called it McGovern's "White Knight thing" (as reported by Gordon Weil in his book *The Long Shot*.)

The experts, the pollsters, and most of the newspapers conceded that President Nixon would be a sure winner in November 1972. On the whole, the American people seemed satisfied with his achievements. As he was gradually withdrawing United States troops from Vietnam, Nixon was expected to bring about a cease-fire in a short time.

President Nixon was so confident of victory in the forthcoming election that, as noted, he didn't even campaign. Covering him was left up to the regular CBS White House reporter, Dan Rather. Because Rather often challenged the president at press conferences, he was considered antagonistic, another reason why Nixon distrusted the press.

Election day finally came in November, and all campaigning was over. McGovern's people had little to encourage them, in spite of the marathon campaign the Senator had conducted. But the reporters who had traveled with him as well as his staff were shaken by the extent of his defeat. Only Massachusetts and the District of Columbia had gone for him. The pollsters had been right. President Nixon was reelected by the biggest majority ever. The effect of such a massive defeat was devastating to the McGovern people and also to the reporters who had covered the long campaign. Even if they were not for McGovern politically, they admired his courage and his gallant fight against great odds.

On the *Zoo* plane back to Washington from Sioux Falls, South Dakota, where McGovern voted, there was an atmosphere of depression. The feeling of letdown had affected all who were involved in the campaign. Some on the plane described that trip back home as one of the worst they had ever taken. When the plane landed at Washington's National Airport that night, it was met by the families of those who were returning. The reunion was marked by tearful hugs and uncontrollable weeping. It was like a funeral, one reporter said.

Connie, who had become, as she claimed, a walking encyclopedia on George McGovern, shared in the sadness of the McGovern defeat. Soon, however, there would be for her an even bigger story to cover.

5

The Watergate Affair

It had been exciting for Connie, covering the McGovern presidential campaign, her first big story, even if she had not been the chief reporter on it. A bigger story for a young reporter just starting out seemed unlikely. But while she was covering McGovern's campaign, the seeds of what would become her next big assignment had been sowed. Shortly after the reelection of President Nixon, the *Washington Post* began to concentrate on what came to be known as the Watergate affair and to feature it prominently on the front page for the next two years.

It all began with a routine police report about a burglary at a big office-apartment building on Virginia Avenue known as the Watergate. At 2:00 A.M. on June 17, 1972, five men were caught after breaking in to the offices of the Democratic National Committee on the sixth floor of the building. The Washington police arrested the five and took them to headquarters where they were searched. One man was found to be carrying an address book with a name that buzzed an alert signal to the *Washington Post* reporters who saw it. "E. Howard Hunt" was connected to a special staff housed in the White House's annex—the Executive Office Building. The two young reporters who immediately made the connection were Bob Woodward and Carl Bernstein. They would become famous before the Watergate affair was over. As crime reporters for their newspaper, the two were used to following up crime stories. Now they investigated the lead from the Watergate break-in and pried it open to reveal further evidence of illegal activities. Soon they recognized the signs of a conspiracy plotted by White House "special staff" and the hired hands used to carry out all kinds of secret, daring acts, such as planting spies and bugging the offices of organizations considered to be the president's enemies. Woodward and Bernstein kept digging and, in the series of articles they wrote for the *Washington Post,* started the unraveling of the Watergate affair.

The burglary attempt was sponsored by a group of adventurous

The Watergate Building in Washington, D.C., scene of the much publicized break-in.

men called the "Plumbers." E. Howard Hunt was one of them. They were paid by a group of wealthy backers of President Nixon called the "Committee to Re-elect the President." The Plumbers' job was to plug the leaks of inside information to the press, among other things. The Nixon staff believed that the Democratic party and their adherents in the federal government were responsible for the leaks. One of the Nixon staff declared that "Democratic appointees are all through the woodwork of this government." Leaking information was considered by some of Nixon's loyal aides to be an attempt to embarrass the president. They proposed doing something—legal or not—to stop it and thus help insure the president's reelection.

For many years, Richard Nixon had treated the press as his enemy and had considered it out to get him. Because of his attitude and his past history, the press returned his hostility. President Nixon certainly wanted the leaks plugged. But later, when the folly of the burglars' and the Plumbers' activities was exposed, he expressed regret. "Because of the emphasis I put on the crucial importance of protecting the national security, I can understand how highly motivated individuals could have felt justified in specific activities that I would have disapproved of."

At any rate, in the year 1972, the Plumbers were very busy trying to infiltrate, for their own purposes, the campaigns of several Democratic candidates for president; later they concentrated on George McGovern, the winner in the primaries, the Democrats' standard bearer. When they directed the burglars to wiretap the Democratic party's headquarters in the Watergate building, the result became history.

Because it was the *Washington Post* that had discovered the burglars' link to the White House, the Nixon people knew that the case would be pursued relentlessly. A cover-up was started. It was feared that the money found on the burglars could be traced to the Committee to Re-elect the President. The FBI would be starting to probe. Accordingly, officials in the CIA and the Justice Department were enlisted by Nixon men to delay the investigation. But the press and the Democratic party then called for the appointment of a special prosecutor and the removal of former Attorney General John Mitchell whom the President had appointed as investigator.

Ron Ziegler, the White House press secretary, tried to downgrade the case, calling it nothing more than a "third-rate burglary." Nevertheless, it was considered important enough for the Nixon personnel responsible for the burglary at the Watergate to form what was later called a "criminal conspiracy." They did everything possible to delay and obstruct the investigation when it was taken over by special prosecutors. They destroyed evidence, shredded documents, tampered with tapes, and when called to testify, several of the conspirators perjured themselves in their attempt to obstruct justice.

As a CBS reporter, Dan Rather often challenged President Nixon during press conferences.

In the meantime, the 1972 election was approaching. For a while, it supplanted Watergate as the big news story. Most newspapers around the country still considered Watergate a Washington, D.C., affair and did not take it seriously enough to feature on the front pages. When the election in November gave Richard Nixon his overwhelming victory over George McGovern, it proved that all of the illegal acts sponsored by the Committee to Re-elect the President were unnecessary. The people had voted their confidence in Nixon and the way he was running the country.

However, with the Watergate mess still hanging over them, and spotlighted constantly in the Washington, D.C., newspapers, the Nixon people were very worried. There were federal grand jury hearings and new indictments coming nearly every day. Once started, the legal machinery of the case could not be stopped. A special prosecutor and a Congressional committee were pursuing the affair, urged on by the widespread publicity. Over the next two years, the Watergate case unfolded piece by piece, revealing shocking acts of misconduct by some of the highest officials in the administration. And all the while, the investigation kept drawing closer to the Oval Office and the president himself. The real work of the executive branch of the government was neglected because of the Nixon staff's concern over Watergate. The president and his men spent most of their time trying to find ways to cover up their implication in the case. Theodore White, in his book *The Making of the President, 1972,* described what was going on in the president's office as "conspiracy, crime and contempt for the democratic process."

Although there were many big names—men in prominent positions in the Nixon administration—who were found to be involved in the Watergate scandal and other illegal acts, there were three whose participation was most shocking of all to the public. John Mitchell, as a former attorney general, was supposed to be the top enforcer of law and order, yet he had helped in the planning of the conspiracy. The other two were John Ehrlichman, counsel to the president and chief domestic adviser, and H. R. Haldeman, chief of staff. It was Haldeman with whom the president was always most at ease. He had been with Nixon for many years and was the one whom Nixon trusted completely. Haldeman functioned, some observers thought, as "chamberlain to the king," deciding what problems needed to be attended to, what messages or documents would be shown to the president, who should be seen. "To isolate him [Nixon] from the trivia . . . that's my job," Haldeman said.

It was further noted that in President Nixon's administration there were only three men who saw the president on a daily basis. Henry Kissinger was one. As director of the National Security Council and also secretary of state, Kissinger was the president's expert on foreign affairs. The other two who saw the president every day were Ehrlichman and Haldeman.

Pressure from the press, Congress, the Democrats, including the defeated candidate George McGovern, grew more intense. When some of the conspirators were called to testify in court, they began to talk. For the sake of their own possible immunity, they implicated others.

Later, practically all of Nixon's most trusted aides, along with the lesser ones, were indicted, tried, convicted, and sentenced to prison terms. The day John Ehrlichman and H. R. Haldeman were indicted was the day the president, according to political writer Frank Mankiewicz, "dropped them over the side." He was willing to abandon them for the sake of his own survival.

"Abuse of power" was the term used by his critics to describe the president's actions. The case went as far as it could, and finally Richard Nixon stood alone, his involvement and responsibility in the various attempts at cover-up made clear. Facing trial in the Senate on impeachment charges brought by the House of Representatives, Nixon resigned the presidency. He was certain that he lacked enough support in the Senate to stand trial and win acquittal, as President Andrew Johnson had won acquittal over a hundred years before.

The Watergate case was closed when Richard Nixon left Washington for his home in California and Vice President Gerald Ford became president. Just a month after he took office, Ford, who had been appointed by Nixon himself, pardoned the former president. That resulted in such widespread outrage that it helped defeat Ford when he ran for election in 1976.

All through the Watergate case, the *Washington Post* kept on it. Having had a large part in uncovering one of the greatest political scandals in American history, the *Post* stayed with the story until other papers considered it worthy of front-page attention. CBS, Washington's foremost television network, helped by giving it wider publicity when Walter Cronkite began reporting on Watergate. Ben Bradlee, the editor of the *Washington Post,* said that the CBS series on Watergate was a turning point. "Aside from a handful of journalists in Washington, the story had not captured the national attention in any sense of the word. The editors all thought it was some kind of weird crusade on our part, but after Cronkite's report, they covered it. Watergate came up to the front pages overnight, and it was Walter Cronkite who did it." The *New York Times* joined CBS and the *Washington Post* in covering the Watergate case exhaustively until it was over.

As a CBS correspondent who had done well in the McGovern campaign, Connie Chung had become quite well known in Washington. Although she still reported mostly for radio, she made it to Walter Cronkite's evening broadcast often enough to become a familiar face on television. Sometimes Connie was assigned to the White House, which enhanced her reputation. She tried, unsuccessfully, to interview Pat Nixon, the president's wife. The first lady, however, was so upset over the Watergate affair that she refused to answer any reporter's questions.

When Watergate became really big news, after Walter Cronkite took it to the television audience, Connie was assigned to it. She was only one of many reporters, from all the networks, who chased after Watergate stories. Even for CBS, she was part of a team, not the only reporter to cover the case. Connie's most important assignment was to cover H. R. "Bob" Haldeman, President Nixon's chief of staff. She also tracked down or "staked out," as she said, other important figures involved in the scandal: John Ehrlichman, the president's chief counsel, John Dean, another key member of the legal staff, John Mitchell, and Richard Kleindienst, who followed Mitchell as attorney general. Connie's assignment to interview these men was an acknowledgment by CBS of her resourcefulness. She herself was proud to be part of the biggest story of the 1970s. She said later that Watergate had "everything—intrigue, mystery, bringing government down." Included in the "unbelievable" story, as she saw it, were "reluctant participants, people who wouldn't talk, staking people out. It was just wonderful, a great story."

When Bob Haldeman, the closest man to the president, was implicated in the cover-up, Connie spent many hours trying to get him to talk to her. Although she knew that would be difficult, she was determined to keep after Haldeman. She had learned, during her campaign reporting, to cultivate contacts who could give her information. She had some sources now in Congress and in government positions, as well as other reporters, sources she considered her very own. They sometimes provided scraps of information that opened up into real stories. It often meant getting her subjects at odd hours, but that did not bother Connie. Ever since she had become a CBS reporter, she said, "There was a lot of waiting for people to come out-of-doors. You just stood shivering in the cold with a little microphone in your hand; the person came out, you quickly asked a question, and that was it. All you have to do is be aggressive; you don't have to know how to be a good interviewer."

Interviewing in depth would come later in Connie's career. When she was assigned to Haldeman and the others, neither she nor the television viewers expected lengthy remarks from whoever was questioned. As Connie said, once she'd asked a question, if the answer came at all, it was only forty-five seconds long. If the subject refused to answer, or was evasive, that did not matter. His attitude, whether cooperative on not, revealed a lot about him. Besides, in Watergate coverage, there was always the next day or the next week. New revelations were coming out constantly.

Attorney General John Mitchell was called by Theodore White "the hardest of all the hard men around the president, by far . . . as

H.R. Haldeman, chief of staff under President Nixon, was interviewed by Connie Chung during the Watergate Affair.

cold a personality as one ever encounters in politics." Mitchell was definitely not about to answer questions from a youthful female reporter. Connie knew that deciding on a successful approach to people is difficult, as well as deciding on how to phrase a question that will bring out an answer. Sometimes, she said, nothing you do will work well. That was true of her attempts to obtain even short, spot interviews with Mitchell. She caught up with him once as he was on his way to testify before a Congressional committee. "I asked him if he intended to implicate the president," she said. He just replied, "We'll have to wait and see." The next time she reached him, she asked Mitchell if the president was involved in the cover-up. He snapped, "You know better than that."

George Meany, the president of the big AFL-CIO labor organization, ignored Connie when she asked him a question about President Nixon. She followed him into an elevator, and he still refused to talk. He left the elevator, as she said, and "never even cracked a smile." J. Edgar Hoover, head of the FBI, wasn't much more cooperative. When Connie asked him if he was going to resign, he said, "The wish is father to the thought." Asked to explain that, he merely repeated it.

Connie refused to become discouraged over unfriendly reactions from some of her subjects. Besides, other reporters who knew her were of the opinion that with her exotic good looks, she could charm anyone she interviewed. "You just have to go up there and smile," they told her about one high official, "and he'll comment." That wasn't always true, but it was noted that many subjects answered her when they would not waste a word with any other reporter. Connie was apt to deny that. Most of the time, she said, after she had staked out a good opportunity for an interview and was ready with her smile, the subject would "smile back and slam the door in my face."

Of her Watergate coverage, historic as the case was, Connie once said that sometimes she was working so hard she felt physically frantic. "I'm a calm person by nature yet I found myself being extremely aggressive in trying to get my stories on the air. And my working hours varied. Sometimes I was outside Bob Haldeman's house at 5 in the morning because he went to work so very early. I'd get up at 3 A.M."

H. R. Haldeman, however, proved to be more cooperative than some of the other Watergate figures Connie interviewed. Several times after staking him out at his home at 5:00 A.M., she got a glimpse of him only as he darted out to pick up his morning paper. So Connie decided on another tactic. One Sunday morning, she followed him to church and waited until he came out after the service was over. Then she cornered him. He was friendly about it, however, and answered a few routine questions without revealing any important information. But her ploy had worked, although she felt remorseful about it, calling it a "terrible thing" to have followed the man to church. Her boss liked it, though, and told her to go out and do it again the next Sunday. Connie says "I kicked and screamed but finally I went out and knocked on his door. Haldeman very nicely agreed to do the interview then so I wouldn't have to follow him to church."

As the Watergate affair drew to a close, Connie tried to get in on some of the Congressional hearings, especially those about the possible impeachment of the president. She would, as one magazine reported, "spring down the corridors of the Rayburn building trying to buttonhole members of the House Judiciary Committee." But when the hearings were finally opened up to television, Connie was replaced by two CBS senior reporters—Roger Mudd and Bruce Morton. They assumed the major on-camera duties from then until Nixon's resignation. A correspondent for another network said, "Connie looks good and she sounds good, but when a major story breaks, they bring in the big guns—the people with experience, with depth."

Connie covered the last days of the Nixon administration at the

White House. On the night President Nixon announced his resignation, Connie said, "Inside the White House, it was like a funeral; outside, Pennsylvania Avenue was lit up by the TV lights, and kids danced and shouted and sang in the streets, a freaky celebration. I'll never forget that night."

The next day, with a horde of other reporters she watched as President Nixon left the White House, accompanied by his tearful family. For the last time, they got in the presidential helicopter that would take them on the first leg of their return to California. Inside the White House, Gerald Ford was installed as the new president of the United States.

When the final curtain dropped on Watergate, Connie said "We all went through withdrawal symptoms . . . nothing seemed quite as significant." The Watergate story, tragic as it was, she described as "far and away the most exciting story of the century."

6

The Rockefeller Story

After Watergate, Connie asked herself what bigger story there could be. It was hard to believe there would ever be another to equal that one. Covering her own assignment in the Watergate story had been "draining," as she said, "running around sticking a microphone in people's faces every hour of the day." But she had really enjoyed the involvement and the excitement.

The Watergate story had also made her a well-known correspondent, especially in the Washington area. Besides being a constant feature on the local news for so long, Watergate was big network news after Walter Cronkite began to take it seriously. Connie won several spots on his evening news program.

Connie Chung knew she had been lucky ever since she had joined CBS. As a general assignment reporter, she had received excellent opportunities to acquire depth and experience, such as going with President Nixon to the Middle East and the Soviet Union. Before Watergate brought him down, Richard Nixon had practiced his foreign policy skills with great success. A large press corps always accompanied him on his several trips. Although at the time, Connie was just one of many in the group, her experiences were valuable and helped her "mature," as she said. She also learned to "take it" whenever she was teased by the other reporters. Lacking their experience, Connie tried to appear extremely self-confident. She tells how one time in Russia a reporter asked her if she was having trouble with the Russian language. She replied airily, "Not at all." "Then what are you doing in the men's room?" he remarked.

Connie's Chinese language ability was helpful when President Nixon's China trip was on the news. She had not gone with the press group that time, but she was asked by CBS to authenticate stories about China that were coming back from the correspondents there.

So Connie knew the score by the time Watergate was behind her. She had learned the rules for getting ahead. Besides cultivating sources, she made friends, whenever she could, with important people, people in power. Her own friendly personality, offscreen as well as on, was an asset in her developing career and helped soften her aggressiveness. Tom Shales, the television critic of the *Washington Post,* said, "She's a tough reporter, very formidable. In Washington, when Connie was coming, you got out of the way."

In May of 1974, Connie received special recognition when she was awarded an honorary degree by Norwich University. For someone who was only twenty-eight years old, this was an unusual honor, indicating her already well-known television importance. In her address to the Vermont College graduates who were mostly women receiving associate degrees, Connie told them "This is the time for women to forge ahead." She urged her listeners to continue their education, mentioning that she herself regretted not having taken the liberal arts courses while she was an undergraduate at the University of Maryland. In covering such complex subjects as Watergate, she said, "I find that I must study and cram just as I did in school."

Connie did not have long to wait for her next special assignment. That was to cover Nelson Rockefeller, one of the most colorful, controversial figures in American politics. Before he could

Connie received an honorary degree from Norwich University in Northfield, Vermont very early in her career.

be confirmed as vice president under Nixon's successor, Gerald Ford, Rockefeller needed Congressional approval. The big story was what the Congressional hearings would reveal about his enormous wealth. "I was on that story from the confirmation hearings on," Connie said, "and I loved it. It was a great assignment. Unlike the McGovern campaign, where I was the number-three person or Watergate, where I was part of a team, I was *the* person, so I felt responsible for him and felt like I really became an expert on everything Rockefeller ever said or did."

Nelson Rockefeller was the grandson of John D. Rockefeller, who had formed the Standard Oil Company in the late nineteenth century. Through that and other holdings, John D. Rockefeller acquired a personal fortune of over a billion dollars. His son and grandchildren who inherited it followed the founder's example by investing on a large scale as well as bestowing huge sums on many worthy organizations. The Rockefeller family became the most powerful dynasty in America. Their interests in oil, real estate, banking, and industry in this country and abroad were extensive.

Their charitable gifts were likewise on a grand scale, bestowed through foundations to benefit education, religion, medical research, and historical and cultural institutions. Rockefeller Center in New York, colonial Williamsburg in Virginia, the Sloan-Kettering Cancer Center, the Museum of Modern Art, and the University of Chicago are just a few of the establishments supported by Rockefeller money.

Nelson Rockefeller, the first member of the family to become deeply involved in politics, violated the family's code of privacy and avoidance of publicity. Starting his career as a young man, appointed by President Franklin Roosevelt to be coordinator of inter-American affairs, Nelson Rockefeller progressed through a series of high-level posts until he reached the governorship of New York, his only elected office. He held that position for fifteen years, longer than any other New York state governor. After his fourth term, he resigned, believing he had served in the office long enough. He had his sights on another political job—the biggest one. He was not secretive about his ambition. "I always took it for granted I'd be president. It was always there, in the back of my mind," he said. At another time, he answered a reporter's question by saying, "President? Well, I'm a politician. That's my profession. Success in politics, real success, means only one thing in America."

However, success in winning the presidency had eluded Nelson Rockefeller. He tried unsuccessfully to wrest the nomination from others in 1960, 1968, and 1972. In spite of his great wealth, his family standing, and his experience in government, he could not gain the support of his own party. The powerful conservative wing of the Republican party preferred the more mainstream Richard Nixon and Ronald Reagan. In addition, as he had once explained, Rockefeller had refused to take years off from his elected position in order to concentrate on running for office, as Nixon had. Rockefeller thought he deserved to be elected because he had been an outstanding governor, because in his many years of public service, he placed his country first. He would not engage in what he called the "mad scramble of nomination politics."

He was, however, as described, a "compulsive extrovert." He relished street encounters, mingling in crowds, even answering hecklers. His own family, adhering to their traditional code, were somewhat appalled by Nelson's openness. His flamboyance and popularity created the publicity they detested.

President Nixon was already under fire in November 1973, when his vice-president, Spiro Agnew, resigned after being charged with accepting bribes. Under the 25th amendment to the Constitution, the president is permitted in such a case to nominate a successor to the vice-president, subject to congressional confirmation. If President Nixon had named Nelson Rockefeller, as he was urged to do by many supporters of Rockefeller, the ex-governor of New York would have become president upon Nixon's resignation. Already, it was considered likely that Nixon would have to resign before his term was over. Rockefeller himself hoped for the nomination by Nixon but was not surprised when it did not happen. Rockefeller and Richard Nixon had never been on good terms, and Nixon refused to put an opponent in line for his own job.

Gerald Ford was Nixon's nominee, a steady, rather stolid middle-of-the-road congressman who was quickly approved by Congress. Ten months later, Ford was inaugurated as president when Nixon resigned in August 1974. In that year of hitherto unheard-of political firsts, it then became Ford's job to nominate a vice-president. He was not opposed to naming Rockefeller, who could bring strength to his own administration. Although Rockefeller had in previous years turned down the offer of the vice-presidential nomination whenever it was offered to him, this time he accepted. As political observers noted, it was the only game in town left for Rockefeller. At 66, his chances for the presidential nomination in future years were nil. As an activist to an extreme degree, Rockefeller had always considered the vice-presidency superfluous, with only one stated duty—to preside over the Senate. A job with so few real responsibilities was distasteful to him, yet he also believed that "Washington is where the action is." He had, years before, purchased a sumptuous home in Washington so he could be near the action whenever necessary. Before accepting Ford's offer, he extracted a promise that he would be a working vice-president with specific duties, and Ford agreed. Rockefeller had hopes of making something significant of the vice-president's office.

Then came the hearings before Congress. It seemed that the Democrats there looked upon this as an occasion to expose the roots of the extensive Rockefeller wealth. The country, too, was curious about Rockefeller money. For four long months, Congress prolonged the hearings that could have been concluded in a week. Rockefeller was as cooperative as possible but finally balked when some Democrats demanded a breakdown of the Rockefeller assets.

He was becoming disillusioned about the position he had accepted. He said he had thought at first "Maybe I can really be of some use. But after all these months, it's lost much of its meaning." He consented to disclosure of the amount of the Rockefeller fortune but refused to reveal how much each of the eighty-four members of the clan—brothers, sisters, children, and grandchildren—owned. That would destroy the family, he said. Congress reluctantly agreed, and the nation had to be satisfied with the public exposure of the Rockefeller fortune as 1.3 billion dollars. That was a smaller amount than had been expected. Rockefeller explained that it had been reduced over the years by taxation, charities, and division among the many heirs.

When Congress finally approved Rockefeller's nomination, he became the vice-president. However, in spite of President Ford's promise, Rockefeller found the vice-presidency to be as meaningless as he had feared. He was offended when Ford made some important decisions without consulting him. Before their term together was over in 1976, Rockefeller announced his departure from politics. In the beginning, there had been some hope that he might get a chance at the presidency if Ford, as it was rumored, resigned before his term was over because of his wife's health. Or he might decline to run in 1976, and that could open the way for Rockefeller. Ford soon made it clear, however, that he was going to run for a full term and also that he did not want Rockefeller as his running mate. He selected Senator Robert Dole instead. Of course, in the 1976 election, the Republican team was defeated by the Democrats. Jimmy Carter and Walter Mondale were elected. Some people thought the Republicans could have won if Nelson Rockefeller had headed the ticket.

After he announced his complete withdrawal from any further political activity, Rockefeller retired to private life. A long-time aide, Joseph Persico, in a book called *The Imperial Rockefeller,* said that as few men could do, Nelson Rockefeller was able to make happen most of what he wanted, "but not what he wanted most."

The background information Connie absorbed as part of her homework made her well informed on the career of Nelson Rockefeller. Covering him was challenging as well as interesting. Rockefeller traveled fast, and that pleased Connie because she was a fast traveler herself. He had a recipe for getting in and out of crowds as quickly as possible, and he offered it freely to other politicians. "Always keep moving, chat, wave, or shake hands, but never stop, even for a second, or you've had it." If Connie herself seemed aggressive while covering him, that did not hurt her in Rockefeller's opinion, for he had often said he liked aggressive people.

When she got close enough to Rockefeller to ask him a question, Connie found that he was quite different from some of the Watergate figures who evaded answering directly. "If you gave him a tough question, he would give a tough answer back," she said. He did not hesitate to provoke the television reporters on occasion and, as Connie said, "would toe the line only part of time." Nelson Rockefeller explained why the newspapers did such exhaustive investigations like the Watergate affair. "Television is hot stuff, you know, with thirty-second and one-minute spots. How else would the poor newspapers compete with them?"

Connie often traveled on Rockefeller's plane while he was vice-president. She was pleased whenever she boarded it and other reporters, recognizing her beat, inquired "What's new, Connie?" When President Ford appointed Vice-President Rockefeller to investigate the Central Intelligence Agency, Connie said she "broke" a few stories about that. After Watergate, the CIA was widely suspected of illegal activities, especially in Latin America. Rockefeller did a good job at uncovering CIA irregularities, as well as heading up some other commissions, which he suspected was a way Ford devised to keep him busy. In performing chores the president assigned him, Rockefeller said ruefully, "I go to funerals, I go to earthquakes."

Connie was sorry when political events turned against Nelson Rockefeller. He had always been very cooperative and friendly with her. He was a good friend of Walter Cronkite and helped get her coverage on Cronkite's nightly news.

Connie's disappointment about Rockefeller leaving political life was partly personal. She had hoped he would be the presidential candidate of the Republicans in 1976 and that she would be covering that story. When it was clear that would not happen, Connie herself thought about moving on, maybe leaving Washington and trying something else in television. Rumors that she was leaving

Nelson Rockefeller was Vice-President of the United States when Connie was a Washington-based CBS reporter.

began to circulate. When Rockefeller heard about it, he invited her to his home for a small party to "celebrate."

The party, held in the official vice-presidential residence, a former admiral's house on Embassy Row, gave Connie a chance to experience the lavish Rockefeller style of entertainment. Although the Rockefellers spent little personal time at their official residence, preferring to live in one of their several other homes, they used the vice-presidential house for all their entertaining. Shortly after moving to Washington, D.C., the Rockefellers had given nine separate housewarming parties for three thousand guests. They held many dinners at which congressmen, senators, diplomats, and other distinguished persons were invited. Tours were given of the mansion, newly decorated by the Rockefellers, and highlighted by pieces of Nelson's famous art collection. For a short time, the old Admiral's House was a very lively place. It was a "real adventure for me," Connie said of her Rockefeller assignment.

Now, with that story finished, Connie took some time to reassess her position. She had succeeded in "Barracuda City," as she jokingly termed Washington. In the five years she had worked for CBS there, she had dutifully covered the stories assigned to her. She had earned her reputation as a capable broadcaster.

Connie had always set goals for herself and, when one goal was reached, moved toward another. Now the timetable of her career seemed to indicate a study of departures and arrivals.

7

California Years

The summer of 1976 was destined to be a turning point in Connie Chung's career. After the Watergate finale and Rockefeller's retirement from politics, other news events seemed colorless. "Everything was boring," Connie said. She was definitely restless and ready for a change. She had never lived or worked anywhere outside the Washington area, except for a brief time when her father's work had taken the family to Houston, Texas. Connie had been a schoolgirl then.

At twenty-nine, she was still living at home with her parents in suburban Silver Spring, Maryland. She was the last unmarried daughter of the Chungs. Connie was very close to her parents and aware that they would miss her if she left. She also knew they would like to see her happily married like her sisters who were established in their own homes with several children among them. They still looked upon Connie as their little sister and were amazed at her boldness and daring in going after difficult subjects for her television spots.

The Chung parents clung to their traditional belief that marriage was the best career for women. They hoped Connie would marry soon, but she felt otherwise. She said she did not have time to get married. She was "always climbing, clawing, trying to get to the next step." She did go out socially with several different young men but would never date anyone connected with her assignments. And that, she said, eliminated a great many people in Washington.

In the course of covering stories, Connie sometimes ran into Maury Povich, her former co-worker at station WTTG. Neither of them then had an inkling of their future relationship. Strangely, however, each would be leaving Washington in 1976 for new positions in widely separated cities.

So Connie was telling herself, "What a boring person I am! What a stick-in-the-mud!" But in 1976, something happened that put an end to boredom. The manager of KNXT in Los Angeles, a station owned and operated by CBS, spoke to the president of the network about moving Connie Chung to Los Angeles. Her job there would be to anchor the local news. Connie was told she could make the choice—go to Los Angeles or stay with CBS in Washington.

It was a difficult decision. There were conditions attached to each opportunity. Station KNXT's news division had slipped badly in the ratings. It was third, behind the other two television stations in Los Angeles, affiliates of NBC and ABC. As the anchorwoman of KNXT (now KCBS), Connie would be expected to raise the ratings. A challenge indeed, but then Connie had always welcomed challenges. In Los Angeles, she would become an anchorwoman— but on the local news. Going from network news to local news was simply not done if one had a choice. Every broadcaster's ambition was to get on network news with its national coverage. Connie was not alone among women in television who were aiming for a chance to be anchor or co-anchor on network evening news. That was the top, the "broadcast of record," as Connie said.

Barbara Walters had made a highly publicized move early in 1976 from NBC to ABC in order to become the first woman anchor of network evening news. Although she left the position of evening news co-anchor after less than a year, there had been comment ever since about who might become the second woman to win such a top-level job. Many people in the television field regarded Barbara Walters' achievement as a breakthrough that would open more doors for women. Connie declared, "I'm ambitious. Sure, I would like to anchor news for a network."

Therefore, the position of anchor—even if on local news—was a lure, and Connie considered it seriously. On the other hand, she had been with CBS in Washington long enough to have made a name for herself. Her ability was recognized by such stern critics as Tom Shales of the *Washington Post*. Words like "determination," "talent," "good looks," and "personality" were used to describe Connie Chung's performance on the air. She could not be ignored when promotions occurred. If she left for Los Angeles, she would be elsewhere if it was ever decided to have a woman team up with Dan Rather or Roger Mudd on the evening news.

Some of Connie's associates were wondering if she was being urged to go to Los Angeles in order to pick up anchoring experience. Connie denied that. She said, "The truth is they told me I'd be better off if I stayed [in Washington]. They discouraged me from leaving and offered me some nice things if I stayed."

The "nice things" that CBS promised could not have included a salary to match KNXT's offer. Some years later, Richard Salant, who was the president of CBS at the time, said he was "heartbroken" when Connie left his company to anchor at KNXT. But, he continued, "I simply couldn't meet the salary that station justifiably offered her."

Connie was earning around $28,000 annually at CBS in Washington in 1976. That was a good salary then, but KNXT offered her $80,000 to start and much more in each succeeding year.

Understandably, that interior monologue Connie listened to kept telling her she was a stick-in-the-mud if she stayed in Washington. She decided she would not forgive herself if she ignored the challenge of a new opportunity. "Here I had this chance to anchor the local news in the second largest market in the United States, something I'd never done before." She ordered herself to "go do it."

Exultantly, when she'd made up her mind, Connie declared, "For the first time in my life, I'm going to do something different. I'm going to California!"

In Los Angeles, Connie's adjustment was not just from network news to local news. California was very different from Washington, D.C. Life seemed more relaxed, people friendlier. The politically drenched atmosphere in the nation's capital, Connie said, made losing an election the worst thing that could happen there. Los Angeles events rated higher on the human interest level, and Connie found that there was a lot of "happy talk" on the local news, something new to her. In the beginning, though, she found it hard to relax, to smile on camera. News to Connie was serious business. After one of her first appearances on the air from Los Angeles, the news director at KNXT asked her to be a bit more natural. Connie tried to loosen up a little and succeeded. It did not take long for her inherent friendliness to emerge.

She did not forget her basic CBS training, however. Her thoroughness in checking out stories, her own hard work, and especially her exhausting schedule impressed the people at KNXT. They learned that as sweet and charming as Connie was, she could be tough when necessary. The word was passed around the studio that in Washington, when it came to getting exclusive interviews, Connie Chung was known as the "stakeout queen."

A typical day for Connie on her new job went well into the night. She anchored several newscasts, starting at 4:30 P.M. when she was sole anchor. On the 5:00, 6:00, and 11:00 P.M. news she shared the anchor spot with Joe Benti or Jess Marlow, whom she called the best partner she'd ever had. She also anchored the several daily 90-second newsbreaks for the Pacific time zone.

After the 11:00 P.M. newscast, Connie stayed in the studio until around 1:00 A.M. She used that time to write reports, read, and take care of her mail. Then she drove home in the small, two-seater sports car she bought soon after arriving in Los Angeles. She did not go to bed until about 3:00 A.M. At home—first a hotel room, then a condominium in West Hollywood—magazines and newspapers were stacked. Connie "devoured" the reading matter, she said, in order to keep abreast of the news. She was a "night person," she declared, and her unusual schedule did not bother her. Back in the studio by the following noon, she stayed there for the next 12 hours although her co-workers maintained that "she was here all the time."

Connie admitted that her work was her chief interest in life. "Work is my consuming passion," she said. She denied, however, that she was a "workaholic" and disliked that label.

Connie behind the scenes checking details of a program.

Working hard helped Connie forget that she was homesick and often lonely. She missed her home in Washington and the closeness shared with her parents and sisters. Although she considered herself all American now, she still cherished the old-world Chinese customs of her home, the food, the language, the principles. Gradually, however, she became good friends with several of her co-workers at KNXT, especially Ruth Taylor, the political editor of the station, and Jess Marlow, her co-anchor. They all took tap dancing lessons together as a form of relaxation. Often at parties, Connie entertained by doing imitations, in particular of Lily Tomin's and Gilda Radner's skits. Her friends agreed that she was a good actress.

One friend, Laurie Burrows, a well-known Los Angeles chef, tried to make Connie feel at home whenever the young newscaster was a house guest. "I make her Chinese noodles and chicken soup for breakfast because that's what her mother used to make for her," Ms. Burrows said. Connie had a healthy appetite, but never gained weight because, as she said, she was always "running."

Fortunately, she had the ability to sleep "on command," anywhere, any time. She always slept on planes, especially if the going was rough. Once in Nicaragua, she said, when she was riding with other reporters in a jeep over possible land mines, she solved the fright problem by going to sleep. Sometimes she would nod off in the middle of a conversation—especially a boring one.

Connie never forgot for a moment that she was supposed to beat the competition and raise KNXT's standing. The other two Los Angeles television stations, affiliates of NBC and ABC, were number one and number two in the ratings. KNXT was number three—until Connie arrived.

The ratings war is a deadly serious game where millions of dollars in advertising revenue ride on the number of people watching a program. When KNXT's ratings began a gradual climb, Connie was given credit for it. She was on the news so much she became a familiar figure, and people recognized her whenever she appeared with a cameraman to cover a story. "Hi, Connie!" was the usual greeting she received. Her smile and obvious friendliness—on the air and off—made her popular. A KNXT reporter, Patti Ecker, said, "When I'd go out on a story and someone would ask where I worked, they'd say, 'Tell Connie I said hello.' " Connie treated everyone well, her co-workers said. She was always courteous and would praise someone who did a good story. She said, "It's nice to be warm and friendly."

A year after Connie joined KNXT, Maury Povich arrived in Los Angeles. He had quit his job with the NBC affiliate in Chicago over a salary dispute. He was then hired by KNXT and became an anchorman with Connie on the 5:00 P.M. newscast. She was happy to be working with someone she had known back home, and Maury was glad, too, to join a friend on the west coast. Connie said once of their short co-anchoring period, "If you blinked, you missed us."

Bad luck seemed to follow Maury at that time. After only six months at KNXT, he left when the ratings of his program failed to improve. Connie, anchoring three different newscasts, was credited with their improved ratings. About the same time Maury left KNXT, his marriage was breaking up. He was "shattered," as he said. With his career foundering, he wondered whether he "should be selling shoes." He blamed himself for the failure of his marriage to a former actress, Phyllis Minkoff, because, he said, he had been putting his career ahead of his family. He was the father of two teenage daughters.

Connie stood by Maury during that difficult period. She "nurtured me," he said, and "kept telling me I should not question my talent." At the time, Maury noted, Connie was the toast of Los Angeles, the "most popular woman on television."

Although Connie dated several men, including some Hollywood movie actors, she never came close to getting married. She said later that she knew from the beginning that if she ever married, Maury was the one she would choose.

From Los Angeles, Maury went to a San Francisco television

station and stayed there for three years. He and Connie saw each other often and became "frequent flyers" on the L.A.–San Francisco route. Then, still searching for stability in his career, Maury returned to the east coast, to a job as newscaster on KYW in Philadelphia. He was there for the next several years. About the time Connie was leaving California, Maury was moving again, back to Washington, D.C., where he rejoined Metromedia station WTTG as host of *Panorama* and co-anchor on the evening news. He and Connie had continued their long-distance relationship during the years Maury was flitting from coast to coast. They would manage once in a while to travel to each other's headquarters for the short time each could spare from their demanding positions.

Connie, meanwhile, was performing extremely well in Los Angeles. KNXT had climbed from third to second place in the news ratings, and first place did not seem far off. Her programs were frequently reviewed by Howard Rosenberg, the *Los Angeles Times* television critic. He said that she was becoming an increasingly dominant anchor figure, a symbol of KNXT's new surge on the ratings scale. By now Connie's face was known all over Los Angeles, her picture plastered on billboards, tacked on the sides of buses. Awards were coming her way. As early as 1977, the Greater Los Angeles Press Club named her a winner in their journalism competition. Her recognition was based on her "best TV reporting for an in-depth study on a subject requiring research." KNXT was mentioned at the same time for "best daily newscast." From the Pacific Southwest Region of B'nai B'rith Women, Connie received a Portraits of Excellence award as an outstanding woman in the media. The chairman of the council making that award recalled the time it was presented. "Connie Chung was beautiful," she said, "and delighted our B'nai B'rith women with her charm and wit." Two years later, Connie received the First Amendment award of the Anti-Defamation League of B'nai B'rith of Los Angeles.

One of Connie's noteworthy honors was her citation from the

Peabody Awards Board in 1980. The Peabody awards are named for George Foster Peabody, a wealthy Georgia banker who gave most of his fortune to educational and social service agencies. Peabody awards in the field of radio and television are called the "prestige awards" of the industry and are likened to Pulitzer prizes in the print media. To win Peabody recognition is said to be the goal of every producer of television programs. In 1980, Maryland Instructional Television, a division of the Maryland State Department of Education, produced a series of programs called *Terra: Our World*. Connie Chung was chosen to be the presenter of the programs, whose overall theme was the impact of current lifestyles on the environment. The problems of world hunger and energy consumption were dramatized on location shots across the country. In presenting the award to Maryland Instructional Television, the Peabody Awards Board praised *Terra: Our World* as an exciting and effective program that was clearly stimulating to young minds.

While she was in Los Angeles, Connie managed to cover the 1980 presidential election and, before that, the important primaries.

Connie won the First Amendment Award of the Anti-Defamation League of B'nai B'rith, Los Angeles.

Connie on location to present the Peabody Award winning television series on the environment.

In connection with the California primary, which she was scheduled to anchor, Connie and Linda Douglass, another newscaster at KNXT, interviewed first lady Rosalynn Carter on the program called "Newsmakers." President Carter was running for reelection that year.

Connie liked to do political coverage and missed the greater involvement in it that her Washington years had provided. She began to realize that as much as she enjoyed her life in California, she longed for the excitement of high-stakes presidential politics and its network reporting. In 1981, when CBS was considering candidates for co-anchor on its morning news program with Charles Kuralt, Connie entered the competition. She had her advocates, especially Ed Fouhy, the CBS news director. He said Connie "would

Mrs. Jimmy Carter being interviewed on KNXT's program *Newsmakers* by reporters Connie Chung and Linda Douglass.

give us experience, perspective, and solid writing." He added, "Connie's been in L.A. five years and that's enough to let some breezes blow through your mind." Diane Sawyer, however, was the final choice of the CBS executives for the morning news co-anchor.

Connie was heavily courted by the two other network affiliates during the time she was with KNXT-CBS. She stayed with KNXT, however, where her salary skyrocketed. At the end of her first year there, she was earning $100,000. Each year the amount rose. By the end of her three-year contract, it was $300,000. In 1980, she signed a second three-year contract with the provision that she could leave after a year and a half if she so desired. When she finally did leave KNXT in 1983, she was making $600,000 a year and was the highest paid local news anchor in the nation.

In Los Angeles, Connie was close to the headquarters of many movie and entertainment television studios. In those surroundings, celebrities were made overnight and often unmade just as quickly. Connie Chung, as someone constantly visible, very attractive, and with a winning personality acquired near-celebrity status. Inevitably, gossip columnists tried to find something in Connie's background that might detract from her reputation. They failed to find anything that could discredit her. The very worst they could say about Connie, her friends joked, was that she went home every night after work.

Nevertheless, in several books and movies, when a hard-driving, female television reporter of Oriental appearance was featured, Connie Chung was supposed to be the model. In John Gregory Dunne's novel *Red, White and Blue,* "Wendy Chan" was assumed to be based on Connie Chung. Although Connie denied all resemblance to fictional characters, she did admit that her work obsession was something like Holly Hunter's in the movie *Broadcast News.* Connie did not worry about her alleged resemblance to fictional characters nor the labels "Dragon Lady" and "China Doll" that had sometimes been applied to her. In real life, she accepted the fact that she was often mistaken for Tritia Toyota, the anchorwoman at

KNXT's rival station, KABC. There was really little similarity, and Tritia was Japanese-American, but Connie was apt to turn their supposed likeness into a joke.

No one could deny that the real Connie Chung was one of the best-liked faces on television. Nor did she deny that she would stop at nothing to get a good interview. It was others, not herself, who described her in glowing terms, mentioning her "cool beauty and crisp authority," her "quick wit," her "seasoned interviewing skills."

By 1982, Connie was beginning to experience those familiar signs of restlessness, the need for a change. Using an expression from her favorite recreational activity in Los Angeles, she said she could feel 1984's special significance "tap-dancing into my heart." She would like to be closer to the primaries, the campaigns, the conventions of 1984—a presidential election year. She said she could see 1984 "coming at me, and I didn't want to sit out another presidential election."

Connie also said that after her several years in California, which she had loved, she nevertheless had the feeling that she was three hours behind. Things were happening all around the country, and she wasn't "plugged" into them. She was asleep when big events occurred in the eastern and mid-west times zones. It was time, as she said, "to come back."

She began making overtures to CBS in New York for a return to network news. She was offered nothing more satisfactory than acting as substitute co-anchor for Diane Sawyer on the morning news. Then Connie decided to negotiate with NBC, arch rival of CBS. Each network's employees referred to "the other network" when mentioning it on the air. Connie's former boss, Bill Small, was now with NBC News, and he offered her a job anchoring the network's early morning newscast, *Early Today,* which was to be renamed *NBC News at Sunrise.* As she was angling for an anchor position, Connie considered this offer very seriously. M. S. Rukeyser, the NBC executive vice-president of public information said, "We think she's terrific. We would very much like to get her."

When she was offered a contract with NBC, Connie accepted it, even though it meant a big drop in salary. $200,000 a year less than she was earning in California was acceptable to her in order to get back into network news. Connie said the NBC offer was "like a bird dropping out of the sky." It was time for another challenge, a return to her first love—political reporting—and the opportunity to do it on a national network. Accepting NBC's offer would mean turning her life upside down again and settling in New York City. But one plus was the fact that she would be nearer to Maury. Now back in Washington, he was adjusting to the stability of being permanent anchor on two newscasts at WTTG. He and Connie would at last be on the same coast, Connie said, within easy commuting distance from each other.

At KNXT's farewell party for her, Connie thanked everyone in the newsroom. She told them, "If it weren't for all you guys, I wouldn't be such a big deal." She said that she had loved it in Los Angeles and she would miss the "peace and quiet," miss driving around in her car, miss her favorite partner, Jess Marlow, even miss being mistaken for Tritia Toyota.

Later, after she had left Los Angeles, Connie said "Time stood still for me in L.A. I didn't age, I had no wrinkles, no gray hairs." On the other hand, Connie said that one of the reasons she left California was that she was getting "fat and happy . . . nothing was making me scared anymore . . . you can't learn anything unless you're scared."

Her success in putting KNXT on the map was heartening, but Connie was not about to boast. To declare herself a success, she said, was presumptuous. "I don't feel there's any plateau where I can rest for a minute . . . I'm always trying to improve. Anyone who stops trying to improve has no future."

8

Rise and Shine

"I love the idea of a new challenge," Connie Chung told an interviewer for *People* magazine in June 1983. That was shortly after she joined the NBC network in New York, having accepted the challenge of trying to raise the ratings of *Early Today,* soon known as *Sunrise.*

The *Los Angeles Times* continued to report on Connie's activities, even though she had moved from California. She had made an indelible impression on viewers in the Los Angeles area, and her departure left a void in local television news. She told a reporter who was following her career that New York was difficult to adapt to after Los Angeles. The hassle of Manhattan was a big shock, she said, compared to the more relaxed environment of the west. "I really feel like I'm a lot older and more worn out from New York."

Of course, she freely admitted it might be her demanding schedule that wore her out, at least in the beginning. "Now I'm on dawn patrol," she explained. That was something very hard to get used to since she considered herself a night person. In her new job, she had to get up at 3:00 A.M. in order to report for work at 4:00

A.M. By lunch time, she joked, she was ready to fall asleep into the pasta. She was constantly on "jet lag."

Sunrise started at 6:00 A.M and lasted until 7:00 A.M. when it led into the older established *Today,* the first and best known of the early morning shows. *Today* had been on the air for over thirty years and had become famous with Barbara Walters as its star. By 1983, however, *Today*'s ratings had fallen from first to third place, and Connie was considered the most likely person to help raise those ratings. As the anchor on the earlier program she would—hopefully—build a bigger lead into *Today.* It was always considered likely by television executives that a strong show would carry its audience right into the following program.

Besides anchoring *Sunrise,* Connie was scheduled to substitute for the network anchorman, Tom Brokaw, on the weekday evening news. She would also anchor—solo—the Saturday evening network news and two or three nights a week would do the 90-second news briefs or news digests that broke into regular programs at different times. It was quite a schedule. Connie took it on without a qualm. She was used to a difficult regimen. Many observers of her career over the years called her a graduate of the television school of hard knocks. In addition to the schedule that seldom even gave her time for her favorite pastime—shopping—Connie looked forward to the 1984 political conventions. She would cover those events as a floor reporter.

The best part of her NBC deal was having Sundays off and being able to meet Maury Povich on those days. Their relationship had endured over the years in spite of the distances between them. New York to Washington seemed a mere stone's throw away compared to their earlier locations. Connie had purchased a spacious apartment in the elegant and expensive Dakota, a New York City landmark building overlooking Central Park. Maury had a condo in Washington. They alternated from one place to the other.

Anchoring the news at sunrise and beating the competition from

Connie on NBC's early show, *News at Sunrise*.

CBS and ABC—that was Connie's number one priority. In fact, Steve Friedman, an executive producer at NBC, said "Connie's career will rise or fall on how well she does on *Early Today*. If it does well, that career could rise a long way." Ever since 1982, when the networks started programming news before 7:00 A.M., there had been intense rivalry among the "big three." NBC's attempt to compete with CBS and ABC had involved the *Today* co-anchors, Jane Pauley and Bryant Gumbel, in hosting, besides their regular show, part of the earlier time program. That had proved disastrous in the NBC ratings not only for the new time period but for its

The famous landmark "Dakota" became Connie's apartment residence in New York City.

follow-up, the *Today* show—thus the challenge to Connie Chung and her willingness to take it on.

The so-called "alarm clock wars" that began before daybreak started because Ted Turner's CNN (Cable News Network) had in 1982 introduced around-the-clock news. The other networks recognized a serious rival who could attract viewers to predawn news and keep them tuned to later news programs. The "big three's" response was to start their own early morning shows an hour earlier with a new name to distinguish them. NBC's *Sunrise,* the CBS *Early Morning News,* and ABC's *World News This Morning* were established as each network's attempt to provide "hard and fast" news to people before they left home for work. After a while, the names for these programs evolved into the more identifiable *NBC News, CBS News,* and *ABC News* all scheduled for the hour from 6:00 A.M. to 7:00 A.M.

The standard 7:00 A.M. to 9:00 A.M. newscasts on the popular early morning shows like *Today* continued their hold on viewers who got in the habit of tuning in their favorites every morning. Besides NBC's *Today,* there were ABC's *Good Morning America* and the CBS *This Morning* show. Later, the Fox Network scheduled *Good Day New York* shown on the local Channel 5. All of these programs have become an established and important part of the networks' news divisions.

The early morning shows gave women the earliest opportunity to co-anchor network news. The tradition then started of having a couple, sometimes called "hosts" instead of "anchors" doing the show. Barbara Walters and her partner, Jim Hartz, were followed on *Today* by Jane Pauley and Bryant Gumbel; *Good Morning America*'s longtime popular hosts were David Hartman and Joan Lunden; *This Morning* had Bill Kurtes and Diane Sawyer together for a considerable time.

The breakfast-time shows, as they are sometimes called, broadcast a great deal of advertising. The filler matter of commercials is liberally scattered through the regular menu of news, weather reports, interviews with celebrities of the moment, film reviews, and special location reports. The messages aimed to sell products are never neglected because the programs depend on advertising revenues. As long as they can claim audience response, the shows' continuance is assured. They are said to attract 15 million viewers every morning, which means 130 million dollars a year in advertising.

Although the earlier sunrise or daybreak shows do not generate as much revenue as the standard early shows, they are relatively inexpensive to produce. With fewer special features, they are said to present more aggressive reporting. They are called by their producers the news indexes of the day—"video newspapers" that let people know what has happened in the world since they went to bed.

The expectation then was that Connie Chung would raise NBC's news at daybreak from the "groggy affair" it was to top place in the ratings. She was to carry the entire program alone, acting as both anchor and correspondent. There would be few if any special reports. Connie herself said there would be no "happy talk and no fluff," just "comprehensive hard news." Her cool, unflappable attitude and professional delivery were likened by one writer to a "bracing cold shower."

This was the second time in her career that Connie was given a faltering program to anchor with the order to strengthen it. She accomplished that with the local news programs in Los Angeles and eventually she did it for NBC in New York. Over her two-year period of anchoring the "dawn patrol," it did at various times rise to the top of the scale or tied with CBS at the top. Connie seldom boasts. But this time, proud of her accomplishment, she declared she took her show from "rock bottom" all the way up. NBC executives were justified in calling her a "valuable addition" to their lineup.

Connie did acknowledge that she succeeded because the show was tailored for her. When Tom Shales of the *Washington Post,* a longtime observer of Connie's career suggested to her that maybe the show was highly rated because she was "so pleasing to look at in the morning," Connie only laughed. Other observers declared Connie Chung was one of the "hottest names in television news."

Jane Pauley of *Today* was granted a three-month maternity leave in 1984 and Connie was one of her substitutes. Then Connie was released temporarily from her early anchoring position in order to report from the national political party conventions. The Democrats met in San Francisco, so it was back to the west coast for Connie. She joined Dan Rather, Roger Mudd, and Bruce Morton in reporting from the floor of the convention at San Francisco's Moscone Auditorium.

In that year, Walter Mondale, who had been vice-president under Jimmy Carter, was the Democrats' front-runner for president. His acceptance was recognized beforehand by the party leaders, so there was not much excitement on the convention floor. Reporters had a hard time finding interesting interviews. They were "scrounging for scraps," as one observer noted. The news executives at the convention moved their reporters around like chess pieces, trying to get something or someone colorful enough for attention.

Connie's most memorable adventure at the convention occurred when the battery-pack she had buckled on in order to use her microphone started smoking. Senator John Glenn, whom she was approaching for a possible interview, noticed it and Connie's futile attempts to unfasten the buckle. He came to her rescue and yanked off the battery-pack, wires and all, before any harm was done. Connie considered it "hilarious" and said facetiously that Senator Glenn had saved her life.

Only when Gary Hart or Jesse Jackson appeared was there some drama to animate things. Gary Hart intrigued the reporters by his enigmatic image. Roger Mudd expressed frustration in pinning Hart down and declared that the youthful-looking senator from Colorado had changed his name, changed his age, changed his religion. Connie Chung opened her report once by asking, "Who is Gary Hart? Many who vote for him admit they have little or no idea what he stands for."

Jesse Jackson was a colorful character who rejected the orthodox style of the old conventions. He worried the politicians because he would not always play their game. But he too was hard to pin down and Connie pursued him in vain trying to get a statement. Then there was Geraldine Ferraro, whose selection as vice-presidential candidate by Walter Mondale electrified—for a while—the drowsy convention atmosphere.

The Republican convention at Dallas later that summer was even more sluggish. Everything was so well orchestrated by the party managers that the nominating convention was called a "waltz" for President Ronald Reagan. He was the unchallenged candidate for reelection. Made-to-order television commercials and films extolling Republican figures took the place of the older live activities and delegate skirmishes. Reuven Frank, NBC's news producer, lamented the new-style, cut-and-dried agenda of the conventions. For that reason, the networks did away with their former gavel-to-gavel (complete) coverage. Only the highlights of the conventions were presented on the evening news by the commercial networks.

The networks' star performers, however, were prominent at the conventions of 1988. NBC promoted its political coverage of the conventions by running newspaper advertisements featuring their top-level reporters on the job at the conventions that summer. Connie Chung's high recognition and popularity with television viewers were emphasized by her appearance with the anchormen John Chancellor and Tom Brokaw in the ads. Connie did not sit in an anchor booth, however. She mingled with the crowds on the convention floor, often sprinted after the celebrity of the moment, trying to get a prized interview. She also made sure to position

Connie reported for NBC at the 1988 political party conventions.

herself in a good spot to snare someone who might have an inkling of a breaking story—for instance, who was going to be George Bush's choice for his vice-presidential running mate? That was the big question at the Republican convention until Andrea Mitchell, another of NBC's correspondents broke that story by her announcement of Bush's selection of Dan Quayle, the young senator from Indiana.

Connie managed a real coup at the Democratic convention of 1988. When John F. Kennedy, Jr., appeared there to endorse the party's candidates, Michael Dukakis for president and Lloyd Bentsen for vice-president, Connie was nearby. She encountered young Kennedy as he was leaving the podium after introducing the keynote speaker of the evening, his uncle, Senator Edward Kennedy. Connie's interview with the only son of the former president, brief though it was, was the first ever television interview granted by him.

However, between the two conventions of 1984 and 1988, NBC had cast Connie in a new role. After two years of anchoring *Sunrise,* she was relieved of her duties on that program in order to prepare for something different. For two months, at least, she would not have to report to the studio at 4:00 A.M. NBC was proposing to start a new prime-time magazine show called *American Almanac.* Roger Mudd and Connie Chung would be the hosts. It is generally understood by television news executives that in order to make profits, a network has to have two assets in addition to regular news. A highly rated morning show and a popular prime-time magazine program are the desirable extras. Every network had one or two or more of these news "magazines," which usually were aired once a week. Described as shorthand versions of the old documentaries Edward R. Murrow had broadcast, the news magazines do not probe as deeply into one subject as their predecessors. Instead, they are usually divided into three shorter segments on different subjects of current interest. They are introduced and narrated by one or more anchor persons. The first and still most popular of the magazine shows is CBS's *60 Minutes*. All of the others from the major networks were based on the format of *60 Minutes*. ABC's *20 / 20* became the next in popularity. NBC had never been able to put together a strong magazine that would rival these two programs. Now it was going to try again.

Unfortunately, *American Almanac* did not arouse enough audience interest after it was started, as the ratings proved. It was withdrawn after a few months to be "retooled" and retitled, according to the producers. It started off again under the name *1986,* still anchored by the team of Mudd and Chung. *1986* was described by Ed Fouhy, the producer of both shows, as more "hard-hitting" than *Almanac.* Howard Rosenberg of the *Los Angeles Times* reviewed *1986*'s debut and said it was much more interesting than *American Almanac.* However, of the later episodes, he said, "*1986* won't see 1987." That turned out to be true. The show ran from June to December, 28 weeks, then it was "axed." Again, low ratings were blamed, and the reluctance of NBC's affiliate stations to schedule it.

The NBC news president broke the bad news to the staff of *1986* at a brief meeting in December of that year. Disappointment was acute, especially for the anchors, Roger Mudd and Connie Chung. Connie was away on a vacation at the time and when she got back to work, it was "awful," she said. She did not know what she was going to do next.

Again, NBC had been left as the only network without a weekly one-hour news magazine program. The news president, however, had mentioned the possibility of starting a one-hour series of single-subject documentaries sometime within the next year. They would span a two-year period and be on prime time. As Connie would learn, she was to be involved in the new format.

It was heartening for her to know that NBC still considered her an important asset. Connie's image, well-known from coast to coast, was really not diminished in any way by the cancellation of her shows. There had been some speculation in television circles that she was considering a return to CBS. That rumor was squashed when she signed a new three-year contract with NBC that reportedly would pay her a salary close to a million dollars a year. Her value to the network was well understood. As an associate of Connie's remarked, "If they lose Connie, they might as well as close the shop down."

The prime-time specials that were to involve Connie Chung turned out to be a true turning point in her career. They were successful and most of them were highly rated. Connie said with satisfaction, "I have no reason to worry about my next step."

9

A "Special" Life

In between anchoring *Sunrise* and starting a new series of magazine shows and specials, Connie had at last found time to get married. When she and Maury were just a shuttle away—she in New York and he in Washington, D.C.—they decided they had waited long enough for a favorable convergence of their lives and careers. In December 1984 they were married in Connie's New York apartment by a rabbi in deference to Maury's Jewish faith.

Connie's parents were happy about the marriage because, as her father William Chung said in toasting the newlywed pair, he had finally married off his last daughter. Maury's parents were proud of their famous new daughter-in-law. They were a media-oriented family, from father to children. A longtime sports editor for the *Washington Post*, Maury's father, upon his retirement, became a sports columnist. Lynn Povich, Maury's sister, was a senior editor on *Newsweek*.

After she was married, Connie declared that "Maury became the most important thing in my life," supplanting her work obsession, which before she married had been her number one concern. That sense of humor, however, which she shared with Maury, prompted her to amend his and her list of priorities. Now, in order, she said they were "my husband, then my work, and then golf." His were "golf, work, and then me." But as a mark of her commitment to marriage, even though a small sign, she had her luggage stamped with her new initials, C.C.P.

Friends of the couple were optimistic about the marriage of Connie and Maury. They believed the pair were perfectly matched, their different personalities blending compatibly. Maury was sociable and open, revealing things sometimes—like her salary—that Connie preferred to keep secret. Connie was the more private one, introspective at times, and as friendly as she was, many of her friends and acquaintances said they felt they didn't really know her.

Connie with her husband, Maury Povich.

Maury, according to Connie, was "sloppy," and she was compulsively neat. But he was learning to pick up things he dropped to the floor, she said, and she was beginning to mislay things—like her umbrella—which she never did before. Maybe it was an improvement for both of them.

Besides their sense of humor, the couple shared other understandings. Similar career backgrounds and hard knocks along the way helped them reconcile demanding schedules and pressures. Their hours together were still determined by timetables and distances apart. They could manage to see each other only on weekends and took turns commuting from New York to Washington, D.C., and vice versa. Connie preferred to do the shuttling back and forth because, she said, "the home team has to stock the refrigerator." The weekend visiting went on for two years. Then Maury obtained an anchor spot on New York's Fox Channel 5. Besides doing the 7:00 P.M. newscast, he presided over another show at 7:30 P.M. on Channel 5 called *A Current Affair.* Ridiculed as "tabloid television" by some viewers because it re-enacted sensational events, the program was criticized even by Maury's own family in Washington. But Connie stoutly defended the show as "terrific" and sometimes helped Maury in going after stories for it.

Maury was catching up with Connie's celebrity. Cab drivers in New York recognized him, sometimes before Connie who was often mistaken for Kaity Tong, ABC's local news anchorwoman. Connie's reaction to that was, as usual, amusement. "We all look alike, you know," she said.

It seemed that Maury might not have to complain any more that Connie was making more money that he was. At least he was getting closer, especially if, as he hoped, *A Current Affair* became syndicated. All or parts of it then would be sold to other networks and could go on for a long time. Popular game and talk shows and sitcoms (situation comedies) like *I Love Lucy, Mama's Family,* and more recently, *Cheers* and *Family Ties* are examples of successful syndicated programs.

As more and more shows are coming into the market for syndication, the buying prices have gone down—to the hundreds of thousands instead of millions of dollars. Still, they are very profitable for the producers of the shows and, of course, the actors who receive their share. Many of these and other entertainment shows are made by outside studios and sold to the networks. Sometimes they are sold at a fairly low price—even at cost—with the expectation that syndication will make up for the low selling price.

Late in 1990, Maury Povich left Channel 5 to look for new challenges. Among the possibilities were a talk show and a national newscast. He published a book that was mainly about his experiences on *A Current Affair,* but was called by a reviewer for *The New York Times* an "entertaining little autobiography." Maury's career took an upward turn in the summer of 1991 when he announced that his new talk show would start in the fall. The "Maury Povich Show" was expected to appear on several stations, having been syndicated through Paramount Television Company.

Another personal milestone in Connie's life occurred in 1987 when she visited China for the first time. NBC News decided to broadcast several programs live from China, and Connie was part of the team that spent several days there. It was an emotional experience for her, and as she said, she cried a lot. She has always cried easily, she admits—over stories, books, films. But meeting some of her Chinese relatives and visiting her grandparents' graves brought forth a really abundant amount of tears. She met her cousins—among them an architect, a professor, and an accountant. She learned first-hand how the Cultural Revolution had affected her relatives. For many years, she and her parents knew nothing about their family members back in China. They couldn't even write because of the restrictions imposed by the Communist government.

Connie's parents, being of the Nationalist party, were afraid of endangering their relatives by revealing any connection between them. Then after President Nixon's first visit to China in 1972, many restrictions were lifted, and communication between the Chungs and their relatives became possible. When Connie finally got to visit her cousins, she was even able to interview them for the NBC evening news.

Of her visit to China, Connie said later, "It was the most rewarding experience I've ever had." She could at last relate her own origins to the history of modern China.

NBC's decision to concentrate on hour-long, in-depth subjects for specials took Connie into a new phase of broadcasting. The aim of the specials was to treat a variety of current problems—or obsessions—in a popular, upbeat way. They required a great deal of preparation, research especially, and lining up the experts or celebrities who would appear on each program. Connie did much of the research and said of her specials, "you live with them so long . . . you become the world's biggest expert on whatever it [the subject] is." It is natural that with the intense preparation required, she would feel she was losing touch with everything else going on. If she was scheduled to substitute for Tom Brokaw on the evening news whenever she was concentrating on a special, she would have to jerk herself away from that to the news of the hour. If she was scheduled to go outside the studio on a certain segment of a special, she would carry a beeper to alert her of a possible breaking news story. As substitute anchor of the evening news for any day, she had to be prepared for whatever might happen suddenly and to deliver an unexpected news event before the other networks, if possible.

Doing the evening news was easy compared to the long-term dedication needed to complete a special. With the news, it is over and done with every day. "It all comes out in the wash each night," Connie said. The daily routine of doing the evening news does not vary. There is the preparation, the meetings with the producers, checking the wire services input. Then there is fitting in the live reports and packaged segments, stitching it all together in the final writing and polishing. By 4:00 P.M. the evening news is almost ready—unless a breaking story bursts in to shatter the carefully built-up assemblage of all the various items that go into the newscast.

The specials, even more than the regular news, require a small army of producers and technicians, none of whom ever appear on television but whose help is indispensable. To do one of Connie's hour-long specials, there would be a team of four field producers, a researcher, a senior producer, an executive producer, at least two cameramen and a sound man. And Connie would be the "straight man," she said, getting the hoped-for responses to her questions. In

Connie Chung on location for one of her NBC "specials."

one special, there might be a dozen interviews with "real" people as well as the big-name celebrities and experts. After the field work and the encounters with the guests, the whole bundle of segments is edited, smoothed, and put together so the seams don't show.

Then when the show is finally aired, a critic calling it "info-tainment" may, in a few words, affect the success of the program. Although she has responded to criticism without losing her perspective, Connie is sensitive to it. But as usual, she tries joking about her reaction. When she reads a bad review, she says, Maury has to go out to their kitchen and remove all sharp instruments.

The first special, which appeared in June 1987, was called *Life in the Fat Lane*. Connie used experts in nutrition to discuss fad diets and their effects. Celebrities who had weight-losing experience, like Dom DeLuise and Oprah Winfrey appeared on the show. That first of Connie's specials proved to be very popular. The series continued, using the same format. Specialists on the subject of each show were interviewed and gave the subject credibility. Celebrities who contributed comment or opinion "dressed up" the program and attracted viewers who might otherwise not have been interested. *Stressed to Kill* was about stress-related illness or trauma. That program included Martin Sheen, the actor, who blamed his heart attack on stress while working on a movie. Joan Rivers contributed an account of her experience with stress.

Succeeding specials concentrated on other contemporary subjects or problems. Not all of the subjects were light, especially one called *Guns, Guns, Guns* about handguns and crime. The documentary special called *Scared Sexless* dealt with the results of the AIDS epidemic on sexual practices. That was the highest-rated NBC News special in over a decade. Celebrities who were called "keen observers of our sexual mores," like the movie and TV stars Alan Alda and Goldie Hawn, made interesting comments. The following specials concentrated on other current situations. The one on aging, called *Everybody's Doing It,* was enhanced by the presence of Betty

White of *The Golden Girls* and Jessica Tandy and Hume Cronyn, the Broadway and Hollywood couple who have been in show business for over fifty years.

Although the specials were rated highly in the market research statistics, some television critics were not impressed. Tom Shales of the *Washington Post* called the special effects of some specials "tawdry" and said that Connie had "sullied her good name" by doing them. To Connie his review was "devastating" because he

Famous actors Hume Cronyn and Jessica Tandy appeared on one of Connie's popular "specials."

had always been her supporter. In spite of a few unfavorable reviews, however, Tom Shales still rated Connie Chung number one in a recent survey of four top television newswomen.

Connie's name may have been tarnished somewhat by her participation in some of the controversial NBC specials, but her value in the market place of television ratings went higher. There is always the popular as well as the critical acclaim to consider. In fact, many critics believe that all of television is programmed for the popular taste—for the people who don't read books or newspapers, who haven't gone to college, or who haven't formed opinions on world events. When Tom Shales said after slamming Connie's specials that it would be hard to take Connie Chung seriously for a while, he was expressing the critical as opposed to the popular viewpoint.

Connie defended the trend to "glitzify" information. She maintained that there is a need to lighten up the seriousness of many subjects, to give them some "flash." The critics may call such programs "info-tainment" and deride this combination of information and entertainment, but they go over well with the average viewer, so the television industry maintains. The specials made Connie better known than ever. Her producers praised her ability to switch from her no-nonsense delivery of hard news to the frothy treatment of the specials. She followed up her new lighter image by appearing on several of the late-night shows. As a special favorite with David Letterman, she proved she could give as well as take. Young people who make up a big part of Letterman's audience and enjoy his breaking of images—real as well as perceived—approve of a big star who does not take herself seriously. They responded to Connie's humor, and she reacted to them. "Let's face it," she has said. "Inside me, there's a stand-up comic screaming to get out."

Besides appearing with Letterman, Connie made guest appearances on *The Tonight Show* and on the situation comedy *Murphy Brown*. The latter, with the actress Candice Bergen portraying a hard-driving female broadcaster, is popular with many real-life women television stars who see in it parallels to their own jobs and lives.

The surest way to determine a show's popularity on TV is by checking the ratings. The ratings do not judge quality; it is quantity they measure, and it is quantity that affects advertising revenue. It seems that advertisers believe their products sell according to the number of people who watch the show on which a product is advertised. If the ratings rise, a couple of million dollars in revenue can be reaped by the television industry. If the ratings of a show go down, and stay down, cancellation of the program is likely. The advertising revenue, of course, pays for the popular television programs. Although television viewers often think their favorite programs are interrupted too often by commercials, the television industry claims that for every hour of television programming there are just seven minutes of advertising.

The oldest and most respected of the ratings agencies is the A. C. Nielsen Company, which compiles statistics that tell what people are watching on TV. Many newspapers publish the weekly ratings scale, and some headline them as "the best and the worst" of TV shows. Nielsen corrects that perception by explaining that their ratings have nothing to do with quality and denies causing the cancellation of a show, as some claim. The company, more recently known as Nielsen Media Research, says that what it does is "count the votes." That is done by means of a small mechanical device known technically as an audimeter but called the Nielsen People Meter by the company. Placed in a selected number of homes, based on a sampling similar to the kind used by the Census Bureau, the meter is wired to the TV sets in a household. Each member in the household is assigned a personal viewing button that by remote control indicates viewing habits according to age and sex. The results are recorded, retrieved, and processed and thus reveal the shows watched by the greatest number of people. What newspapers may designate "the best and the worst" are the shows most watched and least watched.

Another smaller agency that rates television viewing is Arbitron, which uses questionnaires instead of meters. The data retrieved provides an additional way for the networks to assess their advertising charges according to a show's popularity.

A ratings company that deals with several kinds of products in addition to television shows and personalities is called Marketing Evaluation. Its television side is called TV-Q or Q ratings. The Q stands for the quotient of people recognizing a name or show divided by how often the show or person is ranked as a favorite. Technical aspects aside, the Q rating simply tells how popular a famous product is. Polls are taken in connection with census figures in order to insure that the samplings are representative of the

A Nielsen People Meter attached to a family's television set.

99

population as a whole. All income levels, ages, geographical locations, and so forth are considered in the distribution of the poll among participants.

Some well-known persons who have rated high in the Q say that the character they play is what people are rating, not the person himself or herself. For example, Angela Lansbury says people like the character Jessica Fletcher that she portrays in *Murder She Wrote*, not Angela Lansbury. Some actors are not happy about such ratings. It is different, however, with television news stars. They are their own characters. Connie Chung is Connie Chung, not a character in a television series like Bill Cosby or Michael J. Fox who rank high in the Q ratings. A high Q rating for Connie was another plus for her, indicating that of those who merely recognized her, a very large proportion considered her a favorite.

Her NBC bosses agree with the polls. Steve Friedman, an executive producer, explained her popularity by saying that although Connie is serious about the news, as she reports it from her various anchoring positions "she doesn't come across as cold, which is a neat trick." She is not only beautiful, they say, but sincere and natural. That may explain why in a more informal poll conducted by *USA Today,* Connie won again. The newspaper asked readers what television news personality they would like to invite to dinner. Connie Chung was named before all of the other big names of television news, like Dan Rather, Tom Brokaw, Peter Jennings, and Diane Sawyer.

Connie Chung has achieved a status that puts her in the company of Barbara Walters and Diane Sawyer as one of the three most successful and influential women broadcasters. Status is very closely related to the salaries paid to these top television news personalities. Their salaries have been called astronomical, and they are. When people question how CBS could have fired a horde of news division employees on salaries that were mere fractions of the stars' income, the networks defend the practice by citing "familiarity." A familiar face that is likeable enough not to make people turn off the television set is a great asset for a network. The better known a personality is, the higher the salary he or she can command. The anchors of the news get the highest salaries—in the millions, but the correspondents and reporters seen often and regularly each come close to a million. The salaries of all big-name performers are negotiated through agents who bargain hard.

Appearing on network news is a sure way to become well known, coast to coast. Although Connie took a deep pay cut in 1983 in order to return to network news, that gamble paid off handsomely. Her contract with NBC network, over the next six years, put her before the public in several ways—three different news shows, magazines and specials, frequent substitutions for the regular evening news anchorman. Hers became one of the more familiar—and fortunately best-liked—faced on television. Those "sleepless nights and hectic days" as anchorperson, correspondent, reporter and fill-in were well worth it. Her accomplishment in raising the ratings of one failing show—the sunrise edition of the news—did not go unnoticed by the NBC executives.

10

The Anchors

In accepting NBC's offer that would return her to network news, Connie had held out for one prize in the package. That was to anchor the Saturday evening network news. The regular weekday anchorman was Tom Brokaw, who had held the position for almost ten years, and when he was off or away Connie would take his place. That was putting her as close as possible to the top without actually installing her there permanently. Also, she would be in the public eye on a regular weekly basis, much more so than in her very early sunrise show. And she would be *the* anchor. Even on a weekly basis, being anchor was a step up for women broadcasters. They are on local news as co-anchors and on the morning shows as co-anchors or co-hosts. But not even as co-anchors are they visible on the weekday evening network news of the big three commercial networks except as substitutes.

"A male tradition that will be hard to beat," Connie has commented about the chances of a woman becoming one of the highest of the evening stars. She has never made any secret of her ambition to reach that top position in television on the broadcast of record. Her years of experience in all kinds of news broadcasting qualified her for it. Sitting on the bench when she was a youngster in the business, watching the pros, and waiting for her chance to get into the game was the beginning. Her apprenticeship was served in the heart of political life in Washington, D.C. Time spent in the minor leagues anchoring local news seasoned her for greater opportunities. Then back in the big leagues, she endured grueling schedules, hectic switches from one program to another. She was now near the top—but not quite there—as weekend anchor, substitute anchor, special anchor.

If she has ever felt dissatisfied about not becoming a permanent anchor on the evening news, Connie has never expressed it publicly. "I happen to think we have great jobs," she said about women's position in television. That remark was made to Norman Paisner who interviewed her for his book *The Imperfect Mirror.* It was her reaction to a list of complaints some top-level women newscasters made on the Phil Donahue show some years ago. Connie, who was one of the group, said later she was embarrassed by the women's attitudes, and she mentioned all the "perks" they received in addition to big salaries—limos to pick them up, hairdressing and makeup service, housekeepers, secretaries, assistants.

The male tradition that Connie cited about television news started with Edward R. Murrow, the most revered name in broadcasting. In the beginning, he was the CBS one-man news department. As a war correspondent during World War II, he broadcasted from London rooftops while German bombs rained down on the city. When he returned to the United States, he became vice-president of CBS and head of its news division. Radio was Murrow's natural medium, and his program called *Hear It Now* was moved to television to become *See It Now.* That was the forerunner of all the later documentaries, from *60 Minutes* on. Murrow became the most famous television personality in America when he took on, in his broadcasts, Senator Joseph McCarthy, who was conducting anti-Communist hearings in the United States Senate. Because of Murrow,

Edward R. Murrow, the first anchorman, in London during World War II.

despite his controversial commentaries, CBS became the top-rated news network.

In the beginning of news broadcasting, the networks allowed only a fifteen-minute evening newscast. It was considered somewhat unimportant, a filler between other programs. Those who delivered the news were announcers, not anchors. That term came into use during the 1948 political party conventions. A newsman in a booth high in the rafters of the auditorium kept in radio touch with reporters on the floor—anchored them into a team. The name was kept from then on to denote the news person in charge of the evening news.

CBS started the first nightly news program in August 1948, shortly after the political party conventions that year. The other networks soon followed. Until 1948, radio was the popular means of broadcasting news. Some of the big stars of radio, heard regularly every evening, were Lowell Thomas, John Cameron Swayze, and Drew Pearson. When NBC's Swayze was asked to announce the political conventions via the new medium of television, he was not happy about it. But the use of television, crude though it was, proved to be workable in the Philadelphia conventions of 1948. John Cameron Swayze discovered that the politicians willingly climbed up to his booth, eager to appear on the flickering screen of the still unpredictable medium.

Douglas Edwards of CBS found the same thing true as he announced for his network. He and John Cameron Swayze had to ad lib a great deal; there had been very little advance preparation for the new kind of coverage. They performed with the aplomb of seasoned radio announcers.

One of the chief problems in the early days of television coverage was getting the film in time to put it on the air with its corresponding story. The crude machinery of filming and switching from one location to another, besides frequent breakdowns, made the early broadcasts unreliable. The news announcers had to function well in crisis situations.

Four years later, at the conventions of 1952, the year Dwight David Eisenhower was elected president, the improvements in television broadcasting were great. It was apparent now that political conventions depended on television coverage. As television itself was becoming central to American life, it transformed the old-time conventions into media spectacles.

The anchormen of the 1952 conventions were the anchormen of the networks' evening news. Besides Douglas Edwards of CBS and John Cameron Swayze of NBC, ABC was represented by John Daly. At all of the following conventions, the anchormen, assisted

Covering the political party conventions has always been a big part of TV reporting.

by their floor reporters, played an increasingly important role, issuing commentaries and opinion as well as news.

After fourteen years as anchorman at CBS, Douglas Edwards was succeeded by Walter Cronkite. Cronkite had started his career as a radio announcer in Kansas City and from there moved on to wire-service reporter with the United Press International. He was proud of his years of experience as a newspaperman and his stint as war correspondent in Europe during World War II. His long television prominence began in 1950 when he was thirty-four and joined the Washington bureau of CBS. In 1954, he left Washington for New York to become anchor of the CBS morning news and other special, documentarylike programs. Before he became the longest-lasting anchor of the CBS evening news, he had worked his way up in the network and had become an authority on the space program and the Vietnam War. It was under Cronkite's leadership that the CBS network won first place in the breaking news story of President John Kennedy's assassination in Dallas. Fortunately for CBS, one of its reporters, Dan Rather, was on the spot, having gone to Dallas to cover the president's trip there.

In the CBS Hall of Fame, Walter Cronkite ranks right next to Edward R. Murrow. In the course of his long career, Cronkite became friendly with many people in high places and enjoyed ready access to them in conducting interviews for his broadcasts. President Lyndon Johnson always listened to Cronkite's factual, balanced, responsible reporting of the news. When events in the Vietnam War seemed to be going against Johnson, he is supposed to have said that if he lost Walter Cronkite, he had lost the country. After Mr. Johnson left the presidency, he granted Walter Cronkite a series of interviews for television in which he discussed his reasons for deciding not to seek a second term.

At NBC, John Cameron Swayze gave way to the famous team of Chet Huntley and David Brinkley. Huntley's handsome presence and mellow voice, together with Brinkley's dry, dead-pan humor, made the pair the most popular anchormen on television news. They reigned for fifteen years. After them, John Chancellor was anchorman for the next several years. Though a respected and dignified figure, Chancellor always came in second in the ratings behind CBS's Walter Cronkite. Beating that masterful television personality would be next to impossible, as "Uncle Walter" had gradually built up a national reputation and was now considered the top anchorman in the business.

However, after an anchorman has been in the public eye for many years, the networks's top brass begin to look for a change. Those who run the business want younger persons who will appeal

Walter Cronkite, Murrow's successor, interviewed President Lyndon Johnson at the White House.

to a younger audience. NBC found its youthful "symbol of the news" in Tom Brokaw, who had been seasoned in California's NBC affiliate stations and later as a White House correspondent. Brokaw was described by Barbara Matusow in her book *The Evening Stars* as a "smooth operator who almost never made a false step." He was also the beneficiary of some fortunate assets—talent and luck, as well as his own drive and energy. He replaced John Chancellor as anchorman of the NBC evening news in 1981.

At CBS, the Walter Cronkite era was ending also. It had lasted from 1962 to 1981, the longest time ever of one anchor's dominance. The most likely successors to Cronkite were two up and coming younger men who had been with CBS for most of their careers. Each had his sponsors in the politics of the network's hierarchy. Each was attractive, able, experienced. According to market surveys—very important to the executives—Dan Rather outranked Roger Mudd in popularity. When Rather was picked to inherit the mantle of Walter Cronkite, Roger Mudd left CBS for NBC. There he became co-anchor with Tom Brokaw on the evening news for a while and was also host with Connie Chung on several of the network's short-lived magazine news programs.

Walter Cronkite and John Chancellor, after vacating their anchor chairs, became commentators for their networks, appearing at the political party conventions and whenever there were big stories to report.

ABC, the youngest of the big three commercial networks, decided to reorganize the format of its evening news after Roone Arledge became head of the news division. Instead of a single anchor, there would be three—at different desks—across the world. They would be manned by three equal anchors: Peter Jennings in London, Frank Reynolds in Washington, and Max Robinson, the first black anchorman, in Chicago. Various correspondents would handle New York news. From these different desks, there would be shifts of location to other cities and other places. The ambitious new program would be called *World News Tonight.* The face of the news on this network would be more alight with special effects than on the more sedate and slower-paced networks. At first, the program seemed trendy, strange to viewers accustomed to the traditional way of presenting the news. Gradually, however, it became acceptable to the public and rose in the ratings until it tied with *NBC News,* then anchored by John Chancellor. Over the next several years, Peter Jennings, whose basic training had been in Canadian television, became "more equal" than the other anchormen and finally became sole anchor, based in New York, on the renamed broadcast, *ABC Evening News.*

It is interesting to learn that Peter Jennings was first offered the job of anchorman for ABC before the news format was transformed. He considered turning it down, then, because of his own lack of experience. He was at that time only twenty-six years old. But an older ABC anchorman, Howard K. Smith, advised him to take the job. As Barbara Matusow reported, Smith told Jennings, "It's like being nominated for president. You can't turn it down." Jennings did not turn down the offer, although it was some years before he was assigned to cover the London desk as one of the three anchors for *World News Tonight.*

The news anchors really are the evening stars of their networks, much more so than entertainment performers because they are seen more regularly. They are the networks' own, the representatives who are responsible for their owners' news prestige and popularity. Most of the entertainment shows and movies nowadays are purchased from outside packagers who produce the shows, and then sell them to the networks. So it is the newscasters, especially the anchormen, that the networks depend upon for credibility with the public. The qualities the network looks for in an anchorman, besides the basic abilities to communicate and recognize important stories, are personal appeal and "grace under pressure" when there are crisis situations, unexpected breaking stories.

Sometimes it happens that when ratings dip, the news performers are removed, "axed" as the saying goes or, if under contract, moved to another program. A drop in ratings is a very serious event because it may mean that a network will be forced to lower the cost of its commercials.

It is not unknown for one network to try to attract another network's star performers. ABC, by promising even higher salaries and fancier "perks," has lured away several of the NBC and CBS personnel. Barbara Walters was one of the first and most notable broadcasters who went from NBC to ABC for the first million dollar salary. After her, others followed and received comparable high salaries without causing the publicity that her move aroused. There is relatively little comment now about "defections" from one network to another. Harry Reasoner went from CBS to ABC, then back to CBS where he became part of *60 Minutes*. Diane Sawyer went to ABC in 1989 after many years with CBS. Connie Chung herself left CBS when NBC promised more, then returned to CBS in 1989. Maury Povich once said jokingly that Connie was hurt because ABC did not make her an offer. The list is rather long but is to be expected with aggressive agents working for the benefit of their clients—and themselves. *Time,* the weekly news magazine, called the 1989 changes "star wars at the networks."

It is not only the talent or performers on TV who switch to other channels. The executives and producers do, too. When Richard Salant, the president of CBS News was forced to retire, he went to NBC as a vice-president. When William Smith, who was the head of the CBS news bureau in Washington, was rejected for president of the network's news division, he went to NBC, also. Bill Small, who gave Connie Chung her first big break by hiring her at the CBS Washington station, changed over to NBC some years later and was instrumental in getting Connie to switch to NBC.

However, the quality of loyalty to one network is not entirely missing from some of the top stars—the anchormen. Walter

Cronkite was a CBS mainstay; Dan Rather never left CBS even when he was unhappy about some of the decisions there; Tom Brokaw stayed with NBC and Peter Jennings with ABC. If any one of them left the network where he became famous, no doubt there would be shock waves all across the television industry.

Ratings have become so important to television networks that to many people it seems as if the quality of entertainment programs is often sacrificed for popularity. News divisions, on the other hand, are considered by many to be the last hold-out for prestige. Therefore, some recent innovations in news have caused dismay among the critics. News, they say, is being presented as entertainment. The programs called "info-tainment" are examples of this new trend. Designated as news magazines or specials, these programs have used many of the devices of pure entertainment. They have been described by Barbara Matusow as information "with a lot of sugar coating," and they do not go over well with respected critics like Tom Shales of the *Washington Post* and Walter Goodman of *The New York Times.* Connie Chung, while she was with NBC, was involved in helping create as well as host many such programs. Only distantly related to the old documentaries, the "info-tainments" are often compared unfavorably to *60 Minutes,* which is considered the best of the new-style documentaries.

The alternatives to commercial network news, for more and more viewers, are the Public Broadcasting System and the all-news channels like CNN that treat news in a serious way. The *Mac-Neil/Lehrer News Hour* broadcast every weekday evening over PBS, is considered by many as an example of how news should be handled. Both Robert MacNeil and Jim Lehrer, the show's co-anchors, have had offers from the commercial networks that would give them larger salaries. They have refused so far to leave PBS. Both men are comfortable with the greater freedom they have in presenting news their way—without regard to ratings or popularity. PBS continues to broadcast other quality news programs on a weekly basis. *Washington Week in Review* is one. Cable News Network (CNN) also presents daily and weekly programs of news analysis and panel discussions in addition to around-the-clock news. To crown its increasingly prominent role in news reporting, CNN introduced global news in 1988. It now broadcasts by satellite to 89 foreign countries, and American tourists can find it in many hotels abroad. CNN attracted great attention during the Persian Gulf War in 1991 because it continued broadcasting from Baghdad while the Allies bombarded Iraq.

However, in 1989, still another kind of "info-tainment" was begun by all three of the big commercial networks. Simulated news stories, the latest attempt to lighten up news events by dramatizing them, aroused another storm of criticism. Connie Chung, who joined CBS that year, was assigned to host that network's simulated news program.

11

Switching Channels

Early in 1989, many of the notable figures in the big three commercial networks began to circle around in what seemed like a version of musical chairs. The greatest publicity was focused on the women newscasters whose contracts were due for renewal or pickup by the highest bidder. Negotiations between network executives, agents, and talent, as the performers were called, went on until the music stopped. Then two of the best-known women broadcasters, Diane Sawyer and Connie Chung, found themselves in a different network.

At about the same time, the news divisions of the three networks decided to lighten the news by making it more entertaining. The magazine programs would be the vehicles for such modernization. There had been, of course, several "info-tainment" type shows like the ones Connie Chung had moderated at NBC. They did not survive, but they started the trend of simulated news—the dramatization of real events.

Network stars like Diane Sawyer and Connie Chung have a high visibility. It was expected by their new employers that, like Barbara Walters in ABC's *20/20*, Sawyer and Chung would attract many viewers to their programs. They had clout, their salaries were in a class with Hollywood stars, they were compared in value to baseball notables. *Time* called Connie Chung "a power hitter." The shows the networks had in mind would be constructed around their star performers.

The switching of channels began when Diane Sawyer left CBS for ABC. She was immediately scheduled to co-host with Sam Donaldson a weekly magazine show called *Prime Time Live*. Her departure left CBS hurting, so it was said, without a high visibility woman star. CBS began an intensive campaign to win Connie Chung back from NBC. She had left CBS in 1983, of course, for the NBC network because she said, then, that NBC offered her more work. Now CBS offered her more money. Of her salary, Connie said, without confirming the amount, that it seemed "outrageous" and made her uncomfortable. *Time* reported that her three-year contract with CBS would net her close to 6 million dollars.

The symbolic value of attaching a big star like Connie to its network evidently was very important to CBS. She was so well known, a popular as well as long-lasting television celebrity, that she might pull viewers away from the "other" network. As Ted Koppel of ABC's *Nightline* has said, "A familiar face is all that distinguishes a network from the competition."

Connie accepted CBS's offer, although she said it was a tough decision to leave NBC. It was also taking a risk, as some television critics pointed out. CBS had fallen from its former place as the highest-rated news division on television. NBC and ABC vied for first place, and CBS occupied the bottom rung. Since the growth and development of the news services on public broadcasting systems and on cable, many viewers had deserted their former channels. The big three networks, however, still paid the most money to the stars they considered worth it. Their practice of paying excessively high salaries to a favored few has not yet been adopted by the newer channels in television broadcasting, nor is it true in other countries where news is customarily delivered by announcers, not "show-biz" personalities.

The "package" CBS offered Connie, "a marvelous, perfect combination," she said, made her happy because if it opened up as promised, she would be a very busy person. That evidently weighed heavily in her decision to leave NBC because she had always been work-fixated. Many people in the television industry believed NBC had underutilized Connie Chung. Her new contract should remove any grounds for that concern.

First of all, Connie was scheduled to anchor a new prime-time news magazine program, either a revamped version of *West 57th* or a completely new entry. Then she would anchor the CBS network weekend news—a valuable, visible background for a star. Also, she would substitute for the anchorman of the weekday network evening news, Dan Rather, whenever he was off or on assignment. Actually, Connie's responsibilities seemed very similar to those she had performed at NBC, but a plus now was acting as sole anchor on all of her new programs. She was enthusiastic about her contract and said, "This is by far the best situation I've been in."

By the time Connie was on board CBS, it had been decided to scrap *West 57th* and substitute a trendier show to be called *Saturday Night with Connie Chung*. The new magazine would simulate, or "dramatize," as the producers prefer to say, issues of current interest. The CBS executive producer, Andrew Lack, was planning heavy use of simulated news in *Saturday Night*. Connie was excited by the prospect. She said, "This is precisely what we sat down and talked about. This is the reason why I came to CBS." As the name of the program indicated, the show was to be built around her. She would be host, panel discussion moderator, stage manager, voice over, whatever.

The premiere of *Saturday Night with Connie Chung* went on the air in September 1989. The first installment went off well. It was a success, critically acclaimed as a promising audition of the new series. The story of Vernon Johns, a civil rights activist minister in Montgomery, Alabama, in the 1950s, was a new and exciting story. There had never been any significant coverage of Johns before, and with the actor James Earl Jones playing him, the dramatization had strength and substance. Because the recollections of people who knew Vernon Johns were included, the show gained credibility. Tom Shales of the *Washington Post* applauded the good taste and high quality of the program. He said that Connie Chung "made a solid, as well as highly telegenic host," and although the show wasn't journalism, it was good TV. Robert Goldberg of *The Wall Street Journal* went further, declaring in his review that "call it re-creation, call it what you like—I think it works."

Later episodes of *Saturday Night with Connie Chung* were not so well received. In fact, the program seemed to go steadily downhill. In dealing with issues like drug use, political hostages, the death penalty, and nuclear danger, the use of simulated events and actors playing real people aroused widespread criticism. Friends of Abbie Hoffman, the anti-war activist prominent in the 1960s, were upset when they learned how his story was to be told. They claimed it misrepresented his life, and they tried to prevent the program from being aired. *The New York Times* asserted that "Nothing can excuse simulated news," and pointed out that there was a distinction between the old documentaries that were authentic portrayals of news and the "docudramas" that re-created news events.

The use of actors in *Saturday Night* made CBS, so it was reported, the only news division of a network to have casting directors. In the proposed re-enactment of the kidnapping of Terry Anderson, one of the hostages still held in Lebanon, CBS planned to use actors to portray him as well as former hostages who had been released. This took the real participants and their relatives by surprise, as they were not told about the dramatization of the event.

Some were angry about it, others felt it was a way of showing graphically the ordeal the hostages had endured.

In *Saturday Night,* mob action was staged by using ready-made street crowds. The episode on the nuclear melt-down at Three Mile Island made use of some of the townspeople in the staged scenes. Actual places were simulated as well as events. In the Abbie Hoffman story, college students on one campus near New York City were recruited to portray students on the real campus where the action occurred. Posters of the Ayatollah Khomeini tacked on buildings in a desolate section of New York City turned another scene into Beirut.

Blasted by television celebrities like Walter Cronkite and Eric Sevareid as well as newspaper critics, Connie's show was reeling under the attack. Even the former presidents of network news divisions, Reuven Frank and Richard Salant, joined the outcry against mixing facts with fiction. Those who had praised the first episode of *Saturday Night* assailed succeeding shows. Only two months after its premiere, the program was being seriously considered for cancellation. There were questions about whether it could survive after rating eighty-third in popularity out of 100 prime-time television shows.

The New York Times said "It's a terrible embarrassment to CBS News." *The Wall Street Journal* reported that the producers might scrap the reenactments and emphasize real news. That did happen in a new version that focused on interviews and panel discussions of news events. In an interview with Marlon Brando, his first on television in years, Connie was said to have scored a big coup. Although one critic said she did not push Brando forcefully enough, it was understood that he was a tough person to interview. Connie "is just too well-mannered to rein in her guests," said Robert Goldberg of *The Wall Street Journal.*

No doubt there will be other attempts by the networks to devise some sort of winning combination of dramatized news and actual

118

news. Television news magazines that have survived as long as *60 Minutes* and *20/20* may be reexamined for their success and used as models for new shows. A big percentage of the public likes them, especially *60 Minutes.* Also, there are no firm statistics on the public's reaction to the docudramas' mixture of the real and the imagined. Some criticized examples of the hybrid result of mixing fact and fiction, like *A Current Affair,* are likely to be syndicated. Popularity with the viewers is, after all, the networks' most immediate consideration.

Why the networks schedule shows like *Saturday Night with Connie Chung* is related to costs. Because such docudramas are news programs, they cost less than entertainment programs. Shows like *Cheers, Family Ties,* and *L.A. Law* cost the networks, it is estimated, about $900,000 an hour. News programs cost about half that. The actors hired for *Saturday Night* were unknowns for the most part, and their wages were low. Again, if a news program like *Saturday Night* rose in the ratings because of Connie Chung's presence, the network would gain several million dollars. That consideration is cited to justify the enormous star salaries and the risk of investing in docudramas that change the face of traditional news programs.

Even with the show's criticism swirling around her, Connie Chung was regarded as a positive factor for *Saturday Night.* Robert Goldberg summed it up for most of the critics when he said that Connie was a "shrewd choice" for CBS because she is, according to many, "the most likable news person there is . . . with a winsome smile and a delightfully unpretentious manner."

Before the end of *Saturday Night*'s first season, CBS announced a revision of the show's format. Simulated events were out. *Saturday Night* would become a combination of investigative reports and human interest stories. The direction of the revised program was apparent in one of the first that Connie conducted—an interview with Joseph Hazelwood, the captain of the infamous *Exxon Valdez.*

Under Hazelwood's command, that vessel had run aground in Prince William Sound in Alaska and had spilled millions of gallons of oil that damaged the pristine environment of the region for untold years to come.

In his first interview since the catastrophe, Hazelwood did little to justify his alleged behavior, refusing to answer many of Connie's questions. Although he was acquitted of the most serious charges brought against him at his trial, there are still many questions and actions to be explained. Exxon, the company that owned the oil tanker and hired the crew, is considered by many persons to be the prime culprit in the case.

In interviewing Hazelwood, Connie seemed to refute the criticism that she was too gentle in her questioning of guests. She persisted with Hazelwood, trying to get an admission of remorse from him. He, however, seemed to regard himself as a victim. Connie's viewers, by watching the interview, had the opportunity to judge for themselves.

Saturday Night with Connie Chung, however, was due for still more changes. On one of the last programs of the season, Connie announced that she would return in a few weeks as host of a new version of the magazine show. To be called *Face to Face with Connie Chung,* this was scheduled for a more favorable prime-time—Monday evening instead of Saturday evening. Surveys reveal that the weekday evening shows (Monday through Friday) have a higher audience attention than the Saturday evening programs. Connie's new weekly presentation, like most other television magazines, would have the same format. Topics of current popular interest and celebrity interviews would be featured.

In the first weeks of *Face to Face,* Connie dealt with the subjects of puppy mills' abuses and the reclusive life of Greta Garbo, the famous movie star. She conducted interviews with celebrities, notably Cybill Shepherd, the popular television performer. *The Wall Street Journal*'s Robert Goldberg gave *Face to Face with Connie Chung* a favorable review.

The program was short-lived, however, primarily because in July 1990, Connie made a public announcement of her own. She wanted to cut down on her heavy work load, she said, because she was hoping to become pregnant. Several times since her marriage to Maury Povich in 1984 when she was 38, she had been asked by interviewers if she was going to start a family. Usually, she indicated that her career preoccupied her. She had been putting her biological clock on "snooze," as she said. Now at 44, she decided she wanted to have a child, and it was very nearly past time. Her husband was supportive, not only of her long-postponed decision, but also of her announcement of it.

Her decision to cut down on her working hours was explained by Connie when she told a reporter from the *Washington Post* that "There will be times when I cannot work or travel, which makes it impossible to anchor and report a weekly prime-time program as demanding as *Face to Face with Connie Chung*." Connie had, as detailed by the *Washington Post*, in one two-week period, been at home only half the time in order to travel to six different cities coast to coast, preparing for her weekly special broadcasts. The public, of course, does not always realize how much preparation goes into a show that may air only weekly.

Although she continued to anchor the CBS Sunday Evening News, Connie stopped her weekly appearances in *Face to Face*. In place of her show, a new one called *The Trials of Rosie O'Neill* was started by CBS. At the same time, the network, agreeing to Connie's lighter work schedule, announced that Connie Chung would be cutting her appearances to just six "specials" during the coming year.

The newspapers reported not long afterward that it seemed Connie Chung was back working her former six days a week. She was quoted as saying "Life hasn't changed a whole lot, just because it's been hard for me to change twenty years of behavior." But she added "I'm trying not to work like a major maniac." Then in March 1991, she told *People* magazine that she was grateful to CBS for allowing her to lighten her work load and she was willing to take a salary reduction as a result of that.

Evidently, CBS considered Connie Chung too valuable an asset to lose, and was willing to adapt her schedule to fit her needs. Connie herself has admitted that she put off marriage too long because of her career demands. Only time will tell if she also put off too long her desire to "have it all," an accomplishment that many professional women have found difficult to realize.

One of the "specials" she hosted in her limited schedule included an interview with Secretary of State James Baker. This was his first since the beginning of the Persian Gulf War. Connie was notably persistent in trying to get an explanation from Secretary Baker about the United States' failure to give Saddam Hussein the "right" signal regarding his threatened invasion of Kuwait, before the war started. The secretary seemed uncomfortable as he evaded answering directly some of Connie's questions.

Connie Chung's entire professional life has been in television. She is an example of an outstanding career newscaster. Although she has made mistakes and experienced setbacks, overall her image of sincerity has remained. From her beginning as a rookie reporter in Washington, D.C., she knew what she wanted to do and did it, regardless of family disapproval, condescending male attitudes, unfortunate ratings. In a fiercely competitive field, she had to exert determination and drive in order to survive. Over the course of her many years in television broadcasting, she has changed and developed, projecting new facets of her personality. From serious political reporting, she has moved easily to the presentation of the sometimes controversial subjects of her specials. She has absorbed criticism and found it easier to smile more, to laugh heartily, and to hang on with her subjects until she gets satisfactory answers. She can be as formidable an interviewer on occasion as she was a reporter who "staked out" the newsmakers in the days of McGovern and Watergate.

Still one of the most likeable of the familiar faces on the television screen, Connie Chung has herself become a television celebrity.

Chronology

1944—The Chung family left China for America.

1946—On August 20, Constance Yu-Hwa Chung was born in Washington, D.C.

1951—Attended schools in Washington, D.C.
-1965

1965—Entered the University of Maryland at College Park, Maryland.

1968—Worked as a summer intern for Congressman Seymour Halpern.

1969—Graduated from college with a B.S. degree in journalism.

1969—Employed by Metromedia television station WTTG in
-1971   Washington, D.C.

1971—Became a correspondent with CBS News.

1972—Assigned to cover George McGovern's presidential campaign. Accompanied President Nixon with the press corps on his trips to the Middle East and the Soviet Union.

1973—Received an award for excellence in broadcasting from the Chinese-American Citizens Alliance.

1973—Covered the Watergate scandal hearings and interviewed
-1974   several key figures involved.

1974—Received an honorary degree (D.J.) from Norwich University, Northfield, Vermont.

Covered the vice-presidency of Nelson Rockefeller.

1976—Moved to Los Angeles to become anchor of local news at station KNXT-CBS.

1977—Honored by an award for the best television reporting from the Los Angeles Press Club.

1978—Won the Portraits of Excellence award from the Pacific Southwest Region of B'nai B'rith women.

1978—Won Emmys for consistently outstanding television per-
-1980 formance.

1980—Received the First Amendment award from the Anti-Defamation League of B'nai B'rith.

1980—Interviewed Rosalynn Carter, wife of President Carter,
while Mrs. Carter was in California.

Hosted the Maryland Instructional Television's award-
winning documentary called *Terra: Our World.*

1983—Left California for New York after signing an NBC contract
to anchor several different news programs.

1984—Covered the Democratic and Republican political party
conventions.

Married Maury Povich, a television anchorman at WTTG.

1985—Joined Roger Mudd as co-host of NBC's magazine news
-1986 shows.

1987—Visited China with an NBC News team; met relatives.

1987—Became solo anchor of NBC's successful specials.
-1989

1989—Returned to CBS network; anchored several simulated
news programs, which were retooled after widespread criticism.

1990—Announced in July a cutback in her schedule; she hoped to
start a family.

Resumed some of her interrupted programs in November.

1991—Appeared for extended time on the CBS newcasts during
the Persian Gulf War.

Acted as anchor for Dan Rather on the weekday CBS
Evening News when he was away in the Middle East.

Hosted some of the CBS special "magazine"-type programs, such as *Verdict.*

Further Reading

Anson, Robert S. *McGovern: A Biography.* Troy, Mo.: Holt, Rinehart & Winston, 1972.

Bernstein, Carl and Bob Woodward. *The Final Days.* New York: Simon & Schuster, 1976.

Birmingham, Stephen. *Life at the Dakota.* New York: Random House, 1979.

Collier, Barney. *Hope and Fear in Washington: The Story of the Washington Press Corps.* New York: Dial Books, 1975.

Crouse, Timothy. *The Boys on the Bus.* New York: Random House, 1973.

Current Biography. July 1989 issue. New York: H. W. Wilson, 1989.

Major, John S. *The Land and People of China.* Philadelphia: J.B. Lippincott, 1989.

Matusow, Barbara. *The Evening Stars: The Making of the Network News Anchors.* Boston: Houghton Mifflin, 1983

Paisner, Daniel. *The Imperfect Mirror: Inside Stories of Television Newswomen.* New York: Wm. Morrow, 1988.

Persico, Joseph E. *The Imperial Rockefeller: A Biography of Nelson A. Rockefeller.* New York: Simon & Schuster, 1982.

Rau, Margaret. *The People's Republic of China.* Englewood Cliffs, N.J.: Julian Messner, 1973.

Roseboom, Eugene, and Alfred E. Eckes, *A History of Presidential Elections.* New York: Collier-Macmillan, 1979.

Salisbury, Harrison E. *China: 100 Years of Revolution.* Troy, Mo.: Holt, Rinehart & Winston, 1983

Thompson, Hunter S. *Fear and Loathing on the Campaign Trial.* Coronado, Calif.: Straight Arrow Books, 1973.

Weil, Gordon L. *The Long Shot (McGovern's Campaign).* New York: Norton, 1973.

White, Theodore. *The Making of the President, 1972.* New York: Atheneum, 1973.

Index